THANK GOD
IT'S MONDAY!

52 WEEKLY
INSPIRATIONAL MESSAGES
TO BLAST AWAY
YOUR MONDAY BLUES

Book design by Kathryn Nyquist.
Front cover illustration by Zoya Vichikova.

Printed in the United States of America.

First printing edition 2018.

RDC HOLDINGS LLC.
P.O Box 27740
Las Vegas, NV, 89126

www.thankgoditsmonday.life

Mama,

This is for you.

W.

INTRODUCTION

"Do you know what you are?
You are a manuscript of a divine letter.
You are a mirror reflecting a noble face.
This universe is not outside of you.
Look inside yourself;
everything that you want,
you are already that."
— Jalaluddin Mevlana Rumi,
Hush, Don't Say Anything to God:
Passionate Poems of Rumi

For years, I dreaded Mondays. Everything that I did on Sundays had a cloud of fear and trepidation, anxiety, and unease about it. No experience could be fully enjoyed with the upcoming day lurking just around the corner. Monday was a sign of what I didn't want to be doing. It was a sign of unfulfilled dreams, wasted potential, and being trapped in a cycle of unhappiness.

I started writing every Sunday night as a way to encourage myself. It was a way to understand why certain experiences were showing up in my life and how I could be better, stronger, and more in tune with what life was trying to teach me. Somewhere in between the first and last words of this book, I realized that my pain was mostly self-inflicted and my anxieties were based on fears that never actually manifested. What started out as a lesson about finding a way to do what I love became a bigger lesson about living a life that I love.

WHY AM I HERE?
THE PATH TO PURPOSE

I f you've never asked yourself the question, "Why am I here?" then you're not breathing—you're not alive. *The Matrix* is one of my favorite films. The first few times I watched it, I couldn't explain why I felt so connected to the story. All I knew was that Neo's—the main character—search for truth hit a nerve. Looking back, I could say that I was only 14 years old; what did I know about the search for truth? Nothing, but, yet, everything.

What is real? Why are we here? What have we compromised in order to stay asleep or be normal or fit in? Why have we made both self and socially constructed prisons home? However we've gotten where we are, we are the only ones who can get ourselves out and all it takes is a moment of true consciousness. For Neo, the moment his life changed was when he picked up the red pill instead of the blue pill. He chose to wake up and there was no turning back from there.

> "Our job in this life is not to shape ourselves into some ideal we imagine we ought to be, but to find out who we already are and become It."
> — Steven Pressfield, *The War of Art*

What is the meaning, purpose, and value of your life? If you don't know yet, it's okay. What's not okay, however, is just going through the motions of life and being complacent. What's not okay is resting on your laurels while allowing the gifts deposited inside you to lie dormant. If you don't know, then do something about not knowing. Start somewhere: Pick up a pencil and draw something, pick up a camera and photograph anything, read—a lot, write down 1 or 10 ideas a day, push until something sparks inside your soul. Just do something.

> "A child has no trouble believing the unbelievable, nor does the genius or the madman. It's only you and I, with our big brains and our tiny hearts, who doubt and overthink and hesitate."
> — Steven Pressfield, *Do the Work*

Fear is a disease that permeates the depths of the human spirit. It causes procrastination; it requires that you have the perfect opportunity, the right amount of money, even the perfect dream. Fear gives you excuses of why something can't be done and wraps it up in being realistic and practical. Fear robs you of possibilities and you won't even notice until you're on your deathbed wondering "what if…." There is no perfect time to start a business, have a child, or see the world. Life moves as you move; the only constant is change.

It has taken me a long time to understand that "happiness and heartache are inseparably intertwined…without the tragic, the beautiful would be just a frayed strand of half-being" (Maria Popova, *Brain Pickings*). "The experience, not the desti-nation…," I often whisper to myself. When discovering our purpose, it's often difficult and takes a lifetime of practice to embed in our minds that "there" isn't as important as the path there. It takes the same lifetime to understand that the path is filled with dualities—light and dark, joy and sadness, ups and downs. We often discover what we want by experiencing what we don't want. Through it all, it's important to stay the course. It's one thing to find the path and another to walk the path.

> "I don't so much fear death as I do wasting life."
> — Dr. Oliver Sacks

You know who you are. You may doubt that you do, fear what you already know, and go around in circles trying to avoid the inevitable, but deep inside, you know who you are and, sooner or later, you'll have to answer to your calling. When we are told that we can do anything, it's because we can, but we're not here to do everything, just some things. I believe that the source code that runs through this world, forming, creating, and manifesting is the same source code that runs through us. When a flower emerges, blooms, and someday dies, there is no judgment from nature. That flower has fulfilled its purpose—it has lived to its full potential. That is all life asks of us—to live to our fullest potential.

> "Never forget: This very moment, we can change our lives. There never was a moment, and never will be, when we are without the power to alter our destiny."
> — Steven Pressfield, *The War of Art*

There is a quiet, nagging voice that most of us have following us around. It's the voice that asks us to be better, to do better. It's the voice that tells us that we're more than the nine-to-five and two to three weeks' vacation—that we are more than monthly bills and living paycheck to paycheck. It's the voice that whispers "you can do that" when we see someone pursuing his or her dreams. Life wants to know itself through us. It wants to know what it's like to write, paint, dance, sing, heal. It wants to know what it's like to compose a symphony, conquer a mountain and start a business from scratch. It wants to know how deep our resilience goes in the face of adversity. Life knows what we're capable of it's just waiting for us to recognize it, too.

IF YOU DO NOT FEED YOUR SOUL, THE WORLD WILL FEED IT FOR YOU

We're all aware that in order to live a long and healthy life, we have to take care of ourselves. It's recommended that we eat whole foods, exercise regularly, and take vitamins that help nourish us or correct any deficiencies. Focusing on our physical well-being is wonderful, but so many of us forget that we also need to pay attention to our spiritual well-being. I'm not talking about going to your religious/spiritual place of worship every week—this goes deeper than that. I'm talking about feeding, growing, and nourishing the relationship with the God that exists within you.

It's interesting that we constantly think about what we'll eat for breakfast, lunch, and dinner, but we never think twice about what we're feeding our souls. I know people whose souls eat frustration for breakfast, gossip for lunch, and doubt for dinner. There are so many of us walking around with empty, unsatisfied, and completely depleted souls—and then we wonder why our lives are such a mess.

In the morning, you feed your body breakfast, but what are you feeding your spirit? What are you feeding your soul? Are you speaking words of life, wisdom, abundance, and encouragement, or are you letting your soul run on empty? When you're hungry, you'll eat anything in sight just to have something in your stomach, including junk food. The same goes for the soul. When the soul is starved, it is susceptible to the junk energy floating around. There's nothing stopping it from allowing negative thoughts to take root. When your soul is hungry, you're more likely to become angry, depressed, lonely, and unfulfilled.

When I wake up in the morning, the first thing I do is express appreciation for my body, mind, and spirit. I then express gratitude for physical things, such as my bed, my pillow, and all the things that afforded me the opportunity to have a good night's rest. By the time I make my way to the bathroom, I'm back to being thankful for my body. I appreciate the work that it does; I thank it for being so beautiful and strong. From my hair to my eyes to my feet, I create a state of gratitude by acknowledging the purpose of each body part.

When I make my way into the shower, I start to speak words of encouragement and purpose for the unfolding day. I tell my day how it will go instead of letting the events of the day control me and determine my level of peace and happiness. If you do not feed your soul, the world will feed it for you. If you do not recognize and tell yourself who you are, the world will do it for you.

The fact is that no day is ever perfect, but at the end of each day, I know that it was the best that it could possibly be. As I go to bed at night, I let go of all that was and settle into what is. Peace, surrender, and contentment with the reality that all is well flow through me. I awake the next morning and I do it all over again.

When it comes to nurturing and sustaining the power within, one size does not fit all, but the following creates a good place to start:

1. Meditate

There are quite a few misconceptions about meditation. You don't have to be sitting in an ashram in India in the lotus position to reap the benefits of meditation. I use meditation in two ways: to listen and to speak to myself. The goal is to create clarity within. I sometimes meditate for 5 minutes; other times, I can meditate for 30 minutes. I try not to judge myself whatever the outcome is. What's important is that I'm taking some time to connect with the power within.

2. Read, listen, and learn

I make it my duty to know. I live by the fact that knowledge is power. I'm not talking about power over other people but the kind of power that touches and transforms you at the very core of your being. It's the kind of power that causes change — change in the self and eventually in the world. I fall asleep to a book every single night. I play a positive and encouraging audio book every other night. Even as I'm sleeping, my soul is eating.

3. Be present

It sounds so cliché, but it's the one thing I'll continue to strive for until my last moment on Earth. Being present isn't just about the "big" moments. It's about acknowledging every moment, even the most mundane ones. When I wash dishes, I try to really feel the way the water touches my skin; I try to really hear the way the water hits the dishes and the sink. We go through so many moments in this life that we'll never remember. Being present is a sign of respect for where you are and what you're doing. It pushes you to act and not react. Most important, it shows you that life is a gift, not a given.

4. Clean house

Four words: Get rid of it. Toxic friends, old clothes, miserable jobs—If it doesn't add value to your life, get rid of it. Separate yourself from negative people, toss the things contributing to clutter, say no to the things you do out of habit to say yes to something that truly brings you joy.

NOTHING EVER GOES AWAY UNTIL IT TEACHES US WHAT WE NEED TO KNOW

I ask questions. Sometimes, I ask a lot of questions. If I don't know, I ask. If I do know, I still ask because I could learn something. I'm not afraid to ask others questions, I'm not afraid to ask myself questions, and I'm definitely not afraid to ask life questions. I learned at a very young age that there is nothing blissful about ignorance.

"If you don't ask, you'll never know," my mother's voice often echoes in my head. I suppose it's why I find it strange when people who experience certain scenarios over and over again in their lives never stop to ask why.

I'm a big believer in the idea that things don't just happen at random. Life experiences are meant to teach us something about ourselves — to grow us and to mature us. We do not get to move on to the next chapter until we've finished this chapter's lesson and passed the test at the end.

Whenever I talk to someone who says, "I'm not sure why I attract bad guys/girls" or "I don't know why people always take advantage of me," the first thing that I suggest is to look within. The interesting thing is that it's never about the other person. It's always about what's happening within the self. You can't change someone else. The only person you can change is your "self" and that goes for your habits, perceptions, and actions. When you fix what's broken on the inside, your outside experiences start to mirror and reflect that perfection.

It's important to be aware at all times of what your soul is trying to perfect. All you have to do is pay attention and be present to what's happening around you. If you find yourself constantly being bullied, it could be life's way of teaching you to stand up for yourself — and, trust me, the situation will keep popping up until you take control, find some inner strength, and stand up for yourself. If you find yourself in one bad relationship after another, then maybe it's a challenge to start recognizing your worth and realize that you deserve so much more.

Like I said, nothing happens to us in this journey by accident and nothing ever goes away until it teaches us what we need to know.

THREE CRUCIAL STEPS TO TAKE WHEN YOU FEEL STUCK

If there is one guarantee life has to offer, it's that you will face many, many challenges throughout your journey. The size of those challenges will vary and how you handle each one will vary as well. For each of us, there will come a time when we find ourselves facing a challenge that leaves us feeling like we have no control over what's going on in our lives. You could find yourself in a relationship or health rut, working in an uninspired environment, or feeling incredibly undervalued.

You try everything in your power to move forward and nothing happens. You try harder and still, nothing. You feel stuck, out of options, and, more dangerously, out of hope.

Before you settle into desperation and mediocrity, here are three crucial steps you must take to help you get unstuck:

1. Accept

This is a dangerous word for anyone looking for change. It implies that you should do nothing. It implies that you should stay where you are. It implies that nothing will change. I actually view acceptance as one of the most powerful actions a person can take while facing a challenge. Whatever it is you're going through, accept that you are not a victim of your current circumstance. Accept that nothing lasts forever; it will either end or transform into something else. It cannot stay the same. Take comfort in this. In addition, keep in mind that whatever is happening is happening for a reason. Be alert; there are valuable lessons to be learned.

2. Take back your power

As much as life is filled with challenges, it is also filled with choices. No matter how powerless you feel in the face of adversity, you do have the power to choose how you will react. It is always a matter of choice. You choose whether to get out of bed or not; you choose whether you'll go about your day with a smile or a frown. You choose what you say and how you say it. You choose.

3. Thrive

If there is one life lesson that will always be relevant no matter what age or stage of life you're in, it's that you cannot control another person's actions. There is only one person you can control, and that's you. That being said, you need to take your mind off whatever challenge you're facing and focus on yourself. The fact is that you have the power to thrive wherever you are and in whatever your current circumstance is. Choose to be better. Choose to be great. Do this not for anyone else, but for yourself. As Steve Martin says, "Be so good they can't ignore you."

One last thing: Something usually happens in the midst of these three steps — a solution presents itself.

FIVE TYPES OF PEOPLE YOU MUST AVOID TO SUCCEED IN LIFE

"When someone shows you who they are,
believe them the first time."
— Maya Angelou

I live diligently by these words, although I will admit that it took me a long time to implement Maya's powerful words in my daily life. You see, I'm a big believer in second chances. I think people can change if they want to and if they try hard enough. Unfortunately, this doesn't apply to everyone. What I've learned is that it takes a combination of intuition and experience to help me decide who stays and who goes in my life

The beginning of each year brings a wanting of new life and

new beginnings. I relish the opportunity to clean the house and start afresh. My belief is that you can't expect something new to come into your life if you refuse to clear out the old. I apply that philosophy to both things and people. We often hold on to both even when they serve no purpose. The older I get, the more I ask myself if all that is present in my life serves purpose and adds value. If it doesn't, then it's time to let go. Here's a short list of the types of people you may have to let go of to make way for a better and much more fulfilling existence. After a while, you'll learn how to spot these people from a mile away. There'll be no need to get rid of them as time goes by because you'll never let them in to begin with.

1. The constant critic
Those who can't do, criticize. As Benjamin Franklin says, "Any fool can criticize, condemn and complain—and most fools do." Nothing you do is good enough in the eyes of this person. The critic can always do it better and he always lets you know exactly how you should be living your life. The funny thing is that this type of person is usually so busy "helping" you figure out your life that he completely ignores all of the things going wrong in his. There's constructive criticism and then there's criticism that breaks you down little by little until you become a fraction of yourself. Run—don't walk—away from this person.

2. The naysayer
The cousin of the critic, this person is so intimate with the

word "can't" that they're practically one entity. My belief is that those who "can't" should shut up and let those who can get it done. I knew a guy who once told me that "those who think they're the exception never are." He was right. He was never going to be the exception to any rule. I no longer know this person.

> "Whether you think you can, or you
> think you can't—you're right."
> —Henry Ford

3. The drama queen/king

There is always something wrong. Someone is always out to get the drama queen. Life is never on her side. The list goes on. It's important to constantly take stock of where your energy is going. Do you spend most of your day marinating in garbage, negativity, and drama? You may think that an hour in the morning or two hours in the evening on the phone with this person isn't really much, but time adds up and, frankly, you will never get back any of the time you've wasted with this person. It gets a little tricky if this person is family. What's important is that you are in control of the relationship. Don't let your emotions take over and remember that you are not a victim. You always have a choice. If you currently spend an hour on the phone with this person every morning, cut it down to 30 minutes and find something more valuable to fill your time.

4. The frenemy

Does your frenemy love you or does he hate you? Does he want to help you or destroy you? This doesn't just apply to friends and family. A frenemy could also be a boss or a coworker. The frenemy smiles at you and then slowly destroys you. He makes subtle digs masked as compliments. I once had a boss who would compliment me and cut me down in the same sentence ("friendly" giggle included). This is the type of person who pushes you in front of a moving bus and then tries to resuscitate you. Are you supposed to thank them? What you need to understand about this person is that it's never about you. The frenemy's actions always stem from a place of fear. The frenemy needs to make you feel small in order to make himself feel big.

5. The yes-man

The truth is sometimes ugly. In certain cases, it's relative and subjective. It can be painful, harsh, and hard to swallow. It is also freeing. It sheds incredible light on any situation and it is always there—whether we choose to accept it or not. My mother is incredibly honest. She calls me out on my nonsense. When I'm wrong, she tells me I'm wrong. She isn't afraid that it'll create a wrinkle in our relationship. She is also my biggest supporter. She constantly tells me that she's proud of who I am and who I'm becoming. We don't need people who will agree with everything we say and do. We need people who will shine a light on our best and worst qualities and embrace us with genuine kindness in the process.

STOP WAITING, START LIVING. NOW!

I picked up a present for myself the other day: a book by Pulitzer Prize Winner Anna Quindlen titled *A Short Guide to a Happy Life*. It was simple, affecting, and it had one quiet but very powerful message —"You are the only person alive who has sole custody of your life." You might want to start living that life.

My grandfather was a wealthy, self-made businessman. He worked incredibly hard and amassed a fortune. He died without enjoying any of it. I regularly hear stories about the great man that he was. What stays with me is that he was a great man who never lived.

"No one on his deathbed ever said, 'I wish
I had spent more time at the office.'"
— Arnold Zack (*Heading Home*,
Paul Tsongas)

How do you show up in life? Are you just going through the
motions while slowldestroying your souly ? You get to work
in the morning; you sit at your desk for nine or more hours.
Sometimes, you break for an hour. Most times, your eyes are
glued to your screen as you mindlessly chew on leftovers from
the night before. You get home and sit in front of the television. You mumble a few words to your significant other in
between watching the game or checking more work e-mails.
You go to sleep, get up, and do the same thing over again.

"People don't talk about the soul anymore. It's so much
easier to write a résumé than to craft a spirit."
— Anna Quindlen

While you were going through the motions, you missed the
twinkle in your child's eye as she tried to tell you about her
day. You missed the opportunity to get to know the person
standing in line with you at your local coffee shop. You were
too busy scrolling through your phone. Here's another
scenario a lot of people are familiar with. You get up; you
check your e-mail. You eat breakfast; you check your e-mail.
You get to work; you check your e-mail. You leave work; you

check your e-mail. You get to the gym; you check your e-mail. You fall asleep as you check your e-mail.

> "The trouble with the rat race is that
> even if you win, you're still a rat."
> —Lily Tomlin

A 2017 survey released by the U.S Travel Association's Project Time Off concluded that more than half of Americans didn't take a vacation last year. This is sad. Actually, it's tragic. What exactly are we waiting for? John Lennon famously said that "Life is what happens to you while you're busy making other plans." For most of us, we barely even have the time to make other plans. It amazes me that by the time my (Nigerian born) mother was 30, she had lived in Sweden, Germany, Brazil, the U.K., and the United States, just to name a few. She lost her father when she was only 16 and every experience that she had, had to be fought for.

She's now over 60 years old and has been adding an average of three countries to her passport per year over the past few years. There are so many people to meet, so many experiences to have, and so many amazing places to see. What are we waiting for? Many will argue that vacations are for those who can afford it, but what about experiences? Game night doesn't cost much—walks in the park don't cost much either.

"Don't ever confuse the two, your life and your work."
— Anna Quindlen

I spent the last two weeks traveling through Spain. I made no plans about what exactly I would be doing when I got there. For those who know me well, this might come as a shock because I am a planner when it comes to everything, including travel. This time, however, my only plan was to show up. I would show up no matter what. I would show up for the simple moments, the complicated moments, and the adventures. I would definitely show up for the adventures. I laughed and ate my way through Madrid, Valencia, and Barcelona. I met so many incredible people along the way. They had such interesting stories and were so excited to hear about mine. What I did for a living hardly ever came up. Who I was always did.

I showed up and, in turn, life showed up for me.

WHY YOU'RE UNCOMFORTABLE IN YOUR COMFORT ZONE

I recently had a conversation with a friend who has been unhappy at her job for quite some time. The pay is low, the work is never ending, and, worst of all, she feels uninspired. Her story is one that I'm very familiar with. Every day, I meet people who are overworked, underpaid, and, worst of all, feel stuck in their current situation. According to a recent Deloitte Shift Index Survey, 80 percent of people are dissatisfied with their jobs. That same survey mentioned that 25 percent of employees say work is their main source of stress and 40 percent say their job is "very or extremely stressful."

These numbers weirdly make sense to me. They make sense to me because the common thread that exists between every single person that I meet through my job is the need for change. As my friend tries to break out of her uninspiring cycle, she constantly wishes that one day, her pay will become commensurate with the amount of work she's putting into the company. Every time she tells me of her wish, I tell her that it will never happen. "That's harsh," she says. "Harsh, but true," I respond. I don't believe in mediocrity for you and neither does life.

Making more money at a job that is uninspiring doesn't make that job more inspiring. You're still wasting away your potential. If my friend woke up tomorrow and was given a raise, her life would be a little bit more comfortable, but she would also become complacent. The fight and fire that she currently possesses to move forward and change her life would instead become a dim light.

There's a reason why you're currently uncomfortable in your comfort zone. It's life's way of telling you that you've got more in you. It's life's way of telling you to push forward because you're capable of so much more. Don't you dare settle for a mediocre or comfortable existence when you can achieve the extraordinary. It may take a while and you will definitely have some pushback, but it is very much within your reach.

It's time to take stock of where you currently are. Have you lost that fire to push forward and strive for the best? Are you constantly upset that you are not thriving in a mediocre situation? Trust me; you don't want more comfort in your comfort zone. Push forward and strive harder, you are not meant to be where you are forever. One thing that is a given about life is that it is constantly changing. In big ways and in little ways, it's changing.

Life is also filled with many, many steps, each one molding and shaping us for the next. Your current situation is there to prepare you for the next step and, most importantly, to ensure that you are living at your highest potential. Embrace your discomfort and let it drive you to inspired action. We all deserve to be valued and to receive value from the things we spend our time on. We have a birthright to happiness and that includes being happy at our jobs. I mean, we're only going to spend 90,000 hours at work over our lifetime.

FLOOD IT WITH LIGHT

"This isn't who I am." My friend was almost in tears as she was sharing yet another ridiculous work story with me. She was right; the girl who I speak to in the evenings and on the weekends is completely different from the girl who I encounter during the hours of 9:00 a.m. to 6:00 p.m. The interesting thing is that she's not alone. There are so many people who find themselves soaked in misery during the week and fearful of more misery as the weekend comes to a close and a new week begins.

My friend is the most fun, bright, funny, kind, lighthearted soul I know. There is never a dull moment with her. She is optimistic, adventurous, and full of life. Somehow along the way, however, she has let a horrible work situation turn her into someone that she is not—constantly afraid and perpetually sad.

In her defense, she is trying to change this situation. The only answer for her at this point is to find another opportunity and move forward. The frustrating part is that the process hasn't been easy and while she's looking for a way out, she feels stuck. My time as a recruiter exposed me to so many similar stories of people losing themselves in a bad work environment. I've been there myself. I remember asking myself once, "How do you while away time in hell?"

The answer is simple—flood it with light. Once you understand that no one or, in this case, no life/work situation can make you feel less than you are unless you allow it, you can start to shine through whatever circumstance you're currently experiencing. Flood it with light. Darkness cannot exist where there is light. Fear cannot exist where there is light. Flood it with light.

My happy-go-lucky friend has been beaten down so much by her boss that she feels he's smothered the light out of her. My advice to her is to come in extra bright-eyed and with a huge smile on Monday. I have tasked her to bring so much joy to that environment that her boss won't know what hit him. I have made her promise to go the extra mile in everything that she does at work. This isn't to please anyone other than herself. This is her way of taking back control.

Understanding that she can only control her actions and no one else's, my friend is not allowed to leave the office with any kind of emotional baggage. Her boss and workplace are not allowed to rent space in her head for free. She will not suffer at work and suffer some more at home by discussing everything that happened or didn't happen.

It won't be easy. At first, she'll feel like she's faking it, but in the midst of it all, one small, authentic moment of joy will manifest itself, followed by another and then another. Eventually, where she is won't matter as much as who she is. She'll realize that no one can add or take away from who she already is. There will be a sense of peace and then things will change because they always do. They say success is the best revenge; I say happiness is even better.

HOW TO MOVE FORWARD
IN THE FACE OF ADVERSITY

My experience in recruiting taught me a lot of new things over the course of my career. It also reinforced the truth in a lot of beliefs that have guided me for quite some time in my journey. I know with every fiber of my being to always go with my gut when it comes to making decisions. I also know that life and people are guaranteed to throw you curveballs every single day and the only thing that matters is how you react to these situations.

The Lou Holtz quote that states "Life is 10 percent what happens to you and 90 percent how you respond to it" is one that I constantly remind myself of. There are so many things that are beyond our control, but the one thing that we do have control over is how we react to tough life situations. There is no way to prepare for the loss of a loved one, the loss of a relationship, or the loss of a job. Even if you have an idea that any of these scenarios is coming, when it actually hits you, it's always a different story.

So, what do you do when nothing around you seems to make sense, when the life you've built becomes one that you barely recognize? What happens when you find yourself drowning or, worse, completely stuck and you can't bring yourself to muster up even the tiniest bit of hope?

1. Acknowledge what is

There is nothing blissful about denial. You're just postponing the pain that you're eventually going to have to face and deal with. If you're sad, be sad. If, for a moment, you feel like screaming or crying, go ahead and do it. Whatever is happening is happening. It is counterproductive to pretend that it isn't and, quite frankly, the sooner you acknowledge what is, the sooner you can start moving forward with what is to be.

2. Ask for help

A lot of us feel that asking for help makes us look weak. The idea that we cannot handle our lives all by ourselves is unthinkable to most. If this is you, please remember that no man is an island. No matter how strong you are, you cannot carry every burden by yourself. A strong support system, be it family, friends, or a therapist, is incredibly important when you're going through a hard time. Sometimes, it's not about getting advice. You just want to know that you are heard—that your voice and your pain matters. The only way to break through is to open up.

3. Begin again

It may seem downright impossible that what you are going through will pass, but that is exactly what will happen. Time will make it happen, but you also get a say. You get a say in when you move forward and how you move forward. It is your choice to wallow in self-pity or accept what is, pick up the pieces, and begin again. It is important to know that as human beings, we are resilient and we are much stronger than we think. If you can let go of the doubt, anger, disappointment, and frustration that came with being knocked down and dare to muster up just a tiny bit of hope, life will surprise you and meet you halfway.

YOUR LIFE, YOUR JOURNEY.
DON'T PLAY THE COMPARISON GAME

Nothing good has ever and will ever come out of comparing your life with someone else's. This is a fact. It is completely pointless living your life according to someone else's timetable. This is also a fact. So, why do we insist on making ourselves miserable by playing the comparison game?

From Facebook to Instagram, perfect moments of other people's lives flood our psyche every few seconds. We are constantly reminded that someone else is living life better than we are, more richly than we are, and with more passion than we are. It doesn't occur to us that the photos that are currently haunting us have been carefully edited and curated. Out of a hundred photos, one image with the perfect smile, hair, lighting, and angle makes it through. Then comes the editing and, eventually, a filter is slapped on to give it even more gloss.

There is nothing wrong with sharing parts of your life or your passions with people. As a fashion blogger, I indulge in capturing a variety of beautiful moments that I, in turn, share with my readers through several outlets. Unfortunately, things start to go south when we forget that these are just moments or when we start fearing that we're missing out on some grand "life party" and then embark on a journey to prove that we deserve an invitation to that party.

I once read a quote that said, "I hope your life is one day as awesome as you pretend it is on Facebook." No one ever tells the full story—on social media or even in person. What you may not see is that behind the flawless picture of that woman who seems to balance her work and home life so perfectly is a family in shambles. Her husband doesn't even sleep in the same room. That childhood friend who just bought a new house is waking up with night sweats thinking about how he's going to afford his mortgage if he ever loses his beyond stressful job. There is no amount of money or fame that could tempt me to walk a lifetime in someone else's shoes. Why would I want something that was never meant for me to begin with?

No one's life is perfect, so there really isn't any need to compete with someone else's imperfect life. Be content with where you are because you are there for a reason and stop living your life based on other people's expectations or timetables.

Take inspired action every day and create your own definition of success. Be hopeful and thankful. Be happy for others when something good comes into their lives and never, ever covet another person's life situation because only she knows the real story and, trust me, it's hardly ever as glamorous as you imagine.

P.S. Nothing and no one can make you feel less than you are unless you allow it.

HOW TO STOP ANXIETY FROM CONTROLLING YOUR LIFE

A close friend recently spoke to me about an ongoing tension headache. It was always worse on the weekdays and it turned into a full-blown panic attack on Sundays. It was so bad that he could often feel heat emanating from his forehead. My friend is incredibly healthy. He eats well, he works out, and he surrounds himself with good people. He's an all-around happy guy—except, of course, for the debilitating anxiety that sometimes cripples him and thereby prevents him from doing the simplest of tasks.

He knows this isn't normal. I know it isn't normal, and we're not the only ones who believe that feeling this way isn't normal. Over the past few years, I have had friend after friend confide in me about feeling helpless and eventually hopeless. I have felt this way many times as well. The fear of the present, past, and future; the fear of the unknown; the fear of stress; the fear of failure, of unfulfilled potential; the fear of unhappiness; the fear of nothingness—fear consumes us.

Worry, concern, apprehension, unease, agitation, angst...we can mask what we're feeling in as many words as we can find, but I see it exactly for what it is—FEAR. Here's how you move past it:

1. Stop

Be anxious for nothing. "Stop fretting over what will be," my mother whispered to me for years. My mind would immediately respond with the thought that it is easier said than done. The fact is that no matter how many books and articles you read or therapists you speak to, the only way to stop being anxious is to stop being anxious. If I had a friend who kept hitting me in the face, over and over and over again and I asked him to stop, and the response he gave me was "I don't know how to stop," I would look at him like he was insane. I can see myself yelling, "What do you mean you don't know how to stop? Don't lift your hand and don't hit me in the face. Just stop." Sorry to get graphic, but you get the point. Stop fretting; stop thinking about what tomorrow will bring; stop worrying about what others will think. Just stop.

2. Surrender to life

In all of my years on this Earth, nothing good has ever come from me fighting against life's current. On the contrary, all good things have come from letting go. I'm not talking about getting complacent and lazy. I take inspired action when I'm supposed to; I show up when I'm supposed to. The rest is left to a magical force that seems to have my back in spite of what I think when things don't seem to be going my way. I used to think that surrender meant giving up. These days, I know that it means trust; trust in the fact that I am not alone; trust that my journey is not an accident. Most important, it is the knowledge that fear and worry change nothing.

3. Start living

A lot of us still believe in the idea that one day, everything will be perfect; the stars will align and we will finally have the perfect family, home, job, and so on. In that moment, we will be happy. While we're waiting and worrying about when that time will come, life is passing us by. Whenever you find yourself anxious about a situation, ask if there's something you can do to change it now — in this very moment. If there is, do it. If there isn't, leave it. When you start focusing on how you're going to fix the situation or the million ways things could go wrong, you'll only create more stress and anxiety. Let life work for you; let it work things out on your behalf. Go, live, create, be amazing. When it's time for you to take action, you'll know. Remember that if you wait to live your life, life will wait to reward you.

SLOW DOWN. YOU'RE MISSING EVERYTHING

I take the same route to work every day. Every day, I find myself lagging behind some slowpoke who decides that she has nowhere important to be so she is going to take her sweet time driving in front of me. I let myself become agitated. I strategize on how to pass this person, look for an opening to my left, wiggle my way through, and finally get in front. I am now winning. Of course, as soon as I do this, I run into a red light and the person I left behind ends up right beside me. You see, life not only has a sense of humor, but no matter how fast you run, it always has a way of catching up to you.

We're creatures of habit. We know we're creatures of habit and yet it usually takes some drastic event to bring our bad habits to light. The key word here is *usually*. Once in a while, we have a moment of clarity—a bright light breaks through the fog in our minds and a lesson so simple slides into our realm of understanding courtesy of the most mundane life activity. We become present—we get it.

When I drive by an accident, I think of the thoughts running through the victims' minds. Neither the past nor the future matters at that point. Each individual is being forced to face the present moment—to be in that moment.

I think about how much I miss daily on my way to work, all the moments I've surrendered to being anxious about getting somewhere on time. I also think about the millions of activities that I rush through—all to get to a place other than the present moment. We're all guilty of this. In the mornings, we rush through breakfast and traffic to get to work. Then, we rush through lunch to get back to work. After that, we rush home from work and quickly get through dinner, only to repeat the entire pattern again the next day.

Our rush through life not only applies to the workweek. We rush into relationships because we're afraid of being alone (what life sees is that we're refusing the pleasure of our own company); we rush toward unfulfilling jobs because we have to pay the bills (what life sees is that we're afraid of risk). The list goes on...

I believe that we have multiple purposes in life. The big purpose, however, is very simple. We are here to enjoy every single minute of this journey. That is all. It sounds cliché when someone tells us that it's about the journey, not the destination, but we only feel that way because we know that there's truth in those words.

These days, you'll find me singing at the top of my lungs in my car on my way to work or to visit friends and family. I admire the beautiful architecture in my neighborhood as I drive by. Now that I'm aware, I wouldn't dare miss out on the beauty of the sunset before me or the magnificence of the full moon above me. I'll get where I'm going when I get there.

USE WHAT YOU'VE GOT

It's incredible that we spend so much time complaining and focusing on what we don't have instead of focusing on what we do have. If only you had a million dollars, you could finally get your start-up going. If only you had connections in the entertainment industry, you could finally move to Los Angeles to pursue your dreams.

There are so many distractions and excuses around us that it has become normal for us to think that we're missing something. The insane part is that we believe that the "something" we're missing can only be found outside of ourselves.

Fear. It's where a lot of our negative behaviors and actions stem from. We operate from a place of fear so much that we don't even realize what's driving us. The constant comparison of ourselves to others, for example, comes from the fear of not being good enough—of being left out. We channel all of our energy into being carbon copies of other people that we forget that we are each unique beings and that every single one of us, although connected, has an individual purpose to fulfill.

We're like the beggar in Eckhart Tolle's book, *The Power of Now*, who had been sitting atop a wooden box on the side of the road for 30 years, asking for scraps and change. At the request of a stranger passing by, he looked into the box after completely ignoring it for three decades. To his surprise, it was filled with gold.

> "Start where you are. Use what you have.
> Do what you can."
> —Arthur Ashe

What kind of treasure are you sitting on that you're unwilling or too oblivious to recognize? We are each equipped with gifts that have been built, molded, and perfected to fit our personalities. There is no one else better equipped to take your journey as well as you are. Look within. The answer is always within. What part of yourself do you consider insignificant? Is it your ability to nurture people? Or maybe it's your power of negotiation and persuasion. Perhaps it's your ability to make people laugh. What box of gold are you sitting on and completely ignoring? A mother's gift to be able to nurture the next president of the United States or the next CEO of Apple may not be as glamorous as a movie star's ability to transform herself into different characters, but it is no less significant.

The moment you start using the gifts that have been tailored for you is the moment life will start to reward you for stepping up and doing your part. Don't get me wrong; the path is in no way easy. There's a lot of reflection, introspection, and, most important, action. There's definitely a whole lot of trial and error, but at the end of the day, there is no greater satisfaction than knowing that you did the best you could with what you had.

WHAT I WISH I HAD KNOWN ABOUT SUCCESS

Never, ever let other people define what success means for you. I wish I had told myself this every time I started a new job, business venture, or journey. Of course, living in the past does nothing for us. It's how we move forward that counts; what we do now — that's all that really matters.

When most people think about success, the first thing that comes to mind is either money or fame or fame and money — basically, material things. In a world where a person's worth is defined by how many Instagram followers and likes they have and where infamy is the currency du jour, it's not hard to get lost in what society values as successful versus what success actually means to the individual.

In our professional lives, we're pitted and measured against each other. There are metrics that have been put in place to make us feel bigger or smaller than others. The same thing applies to life outside of work. We have set up metrics as a society to make us feel like we are better than or worse off than our friends, families, and even strangers. No matter how rich, powerful, strong, intelligent, and ambitious you are, there's always someone else who's slightly ahead. Someone is always keeping score. Speaking of societal metrics, if you're still single at a certain age, then you're a lonely failure. If you refuse to have kids, you deserve pity. If you choose to travel the world instead of staying put and taking on a mortgage, then you're a nomad with no roots or foundation.

We often forget that we're not here to live other people's lives. We entered this world as individuals, not as a group, so why do we put so much emphasis on what the group values? Why are we so afraid to make our own rules or, even better, live without rules? Therapist and Yogi Tara Brach provides an insightful answer to this inner turmoil. Quoting Mother Teresa, she states, "The biggest disease today is not leprosy or tuberculosis but rather the feeling of not belonging." Could it really be as simple as the fear of being left out? In a society that screams for individuality and self-expression, how is it possible that the moment someone decides to take the path less traveled, he/she becomes ostracized?

My mother was a full-time mom of six as well as a full-time

entrepreneur. Success to her meant raising healthy, well-adjusted kids. It meant every single one of her kids graduating from college. Her business thrived, but that came second. Success to some people could be as simple as getting up in the morning. To others, it's having the freedom to choose who and what they spend their time on. What is enough or plentiful differs from one person to another.

I've often spoken about the need to recognize that this is your journey, your life, filled with your decisions, which means you should get to define your successes. Perhaps it's completing the first chapter of that book you've dreamed of writing for years, or maybe it's quitting your job to backpack through South America. It's time we stop defining life's moments as big or small. Each milestone and achievement is equally powerful because each gets us closer to realizing the fullness of who we are. Growth is growth, be it an inch or a mile. Our achievements matter because we say they matter; we are successful because we say we are.

JUST SAY NO

M uch has been said about the power of the word *no*, yet most of us still find ourselves unable to utter this word with the same ease that we possess when we say *yes* to something or someone. We say yes to so many things we wish we didn't. We overextend ourselves, make promises we can't keep, and value other people's opinions over our own. By saying yes to all these things, we miss the fact that we're actually saying *no* to the one thing that matters the most—ourselves.

The word itself is not hard to say, yet it creates an inner battle and turmoil within most of us. To speak it aloud leaves us with an overwhelming feeling of guilt. We feel that by saying no, we're letting people down. We'd rather say yes and be unhappy than risk someone looking at us with disappointment and judgment.

We can talk about the many reasons why we are the way we are *or* we can be better. It's time to gain a little self-respect and, in the words of one of my favorite authors, James Altucher, "choose ourselves." That means saying no to crappy friends, nosy people, rude coworkers, unfulfilling relationships, mediocre company, and mindless conversations.

You actually don't need to explain your reason behind saying no. This is your life. The choices that come up in your journey are yours to make. You owe no one an explanation for the path you choose to take. Be kind, be thoughtful, be charitable, but please remember that charity begins at home and home begins with you.

IT DOESN'T MATTER

I recently overheard an intimate conversation between two young ladies at a coffee shop that I frequent. It was about a major life decision that one of them had just made. I listened as the girl behind me fumbled her way through the many reasons why this decision was the best thing for her. Her friend didn't say much, but I could sense the tension and judgment in the air. I'm guessing the girl behind me sensed it, too, because the explanations, like verbal diarrhea, just kept coming. I felt bad for her. I wanted to reach over, squeeze her hand, and tell her that it didn't matter.

"It doesn't matter." I find myself repeating this a lot. I'll keep repeating it until I completely break free of every need to explain myself to others. It's not an easy task, but it has gotten easier.

> "When you come right down to it, opinions are
> the most superficial things about anyone."
> —Jorge Luis Borgas

I learned at a very young age that it takes a certain kind of bravery to stop caring about what others think of you. I learned later in life that it takes the same amount of bravery to stop the constant need to explain your journey and your decisions to others. For every decision you make and every supporter you gain, there are detractors and naysayers telling you that they would have done things differently.

> "Your opinion of me is none of my business."
> —Judy Ford

You can't ever stop someone from forming opinions about you. Quite frankly, it's exhausting trying to mold the way people see you. It's okay if people don't like you; it's okay if people don't agree with your decisions; it's also okay if people don't believe in your dreams. We focus so much on the destination instead of the journey that we become paralyzed at the prospect of making the wrong move. We let other people's voices into our heads and we soak ourselves in their judgments and opinions. In the end, we find ourselves answering to everyone else but ourselves. What a sad way to live.

Not caring what others think of you takes a certain kind of bravery indeed. It is not something that comes naturally to most of us, but it is a skill that we can all cultivate. What I find is that every time I exercise this skill, I feel lighter and freer. I feel like myself. Isn't that all we really want?

YOUR INTUITION—THE MOST POWERFUL TOOL YOU'RE NOT USING

My intuition has never led me astray. I've known this since I was about eight years old. The only times I've gotten into trouble were when I blatantly went against it. The importance of knowing this didn't really hit me until much later. It turns out that life has a way of making you feel like you've been dumped on an island with the expectation that you just have to figure things out.

In the midst of feeling lost and stranded, you start to take some action, hoping that everything will come out okay. When things don't come out okay, you ask yourself if your fate is set. Do your choices even matter? You start searching for tools to help you make sense of where you are, of why you are, and, most important, of what it all means. Eventually, you realize that, of course, you weren't just dumped here. You start understanding that you are neither a victim of circumstance nor fate. You are most certainly not a slave to the environment you're in. As you dig deeper, you realize that there are, indeed, several tools that have been put in place to help you figure things out, to help you become the fullest version of yourself.

> "The intuitive mind is a sacred gift and the rational mind is a faithful servant. We have created a society that honors the servant and has forgotten the gift."
> — Anonymous

Intuition, sixth sense, hunch, gut feeling…it guides you away from certain things and drives you toward others. You meet someone and something about her doesn't agree with you — something's off. There's a deal on the table, but you sense something isn't right; maybe you should wait. For some, the voice is soft, almost like a whisper. For others, it's firm and all-knowing. You can't explain it; you don't need proof, evidence, or reasoning — you just know.

We are all intuitive by nature. It is one of the most powerful gifts that we've each been given on our journey and, like a muscle, the more you use it, the stronger it becomes. Making this gift work for you also requires trust. I'm not talking about trust in other people's opinions, actions, and advice, but complete and utter trust in yourself. It's the only way this can work.

> "Trust your hunches. They're usually based on facts
> filed away just below the conscious level."
> — Joyce Brothers

Take the job, don't take the job; move away, don't move away; marry him/her, don't marry him/her. We will always be presented with important moments where we need absolute clarity and truth to make a decision. *C'est la vie*. These days, I find that I rarely ask myself, "What do you think?" but rather, "What do you know?"

My intuition has never led me astray. The only times I've gotten into trouble were when I blatantly went against it.

WHAT DO YOU THINK YOU'RE WORTH?

Years ago, a headhunter reached out to me about a potential job opportunity. I wasn't actively looking, but she felt the job would be the perfect next step in my career. We talked about the salary range for the role and then she asked me what I was looking for—a very common question. I went on a rant about where I was and where I thought I should/could be. I was basically trying to justify my value to her. She listened intently and then she said nothing. A moment later, she asked "Wemi, what do you think you're worth?"

I was stunned. It wasn't the most mind-blowing question I'd ever been asked, but it blew my mind in that moment. As human beings, we spend so much time justifying our quirks, wants, and needs (basically our entire existence) to the world that it never occurs to us to have a conversation with ourselves about our own value.

Recognizing one's worth is not just tied to money. When it comes to your time or even relationships, what do you think you're worth? Is it a friend who only remembers you exist when he needs something? Or perhaps it's a job that takes up so much of your time that it has drained you of the ability to have outside interests, friends, or hobbies. What do you think you're worth?

Look around and take stock. The things that exist in your life are things you've said *yes* to, be it consciously or unconsciously. You are not a victim of circumstance. The fact is that most of us don't spend enough time really getting to know who we are. We forget that when you truly know yourself, you understand your value as well. When you know your value, not only will you be able to stand strong in what you have to offer as a human being, you'll feel confident walking away if other people don't share in that vision.

Dare to ask for more. Hold out for a meaningful relationship instead of a space filler. Do things that make you feel uncomfortable but add to your growth and self-worth. Don't be afraid to have tough conversations—especially with yourself. If you don't make a decision on what you're worth, the world will decide for you.

WORKPLACE POLITICS: HOW TO STAY OUT OF IT

Politics are everywhere: at work, within families, friendships, schools, everywhere. I've seen more politics at play within some families than at our nation's capital. What I've learned is that it's not really about the politics itself, it's about people. We have politics everywhere because we have people everywhere. It's easy to avoid all drama, but it's not so easy to avoid all people.

I often say that the most important lesson I've mastered about people is that you cannot control what they do, how they act, or what they say. The only person you can control is yourself. Then, I suppose it's not really about people — it's about you.

Here's what you can do to avoid drama in the workplace and a lot of other situations.

"Your opinion of me is none of my business"

It is my belief that when others speak badly of you, it's a reflection of who they are and not who you are. I stand strongly on the motto that other people's opinions of me are none of my business. It's difficult to do, but it's important that you train yourself not to get emotionally involved and invested in human drama. Narratives change; emotions run high and low. In being still, you can avoid getting involved and the trauma that follows.

"If you don't have anything nice to say,
don't say anything at all."

You've heard this so many times, but sometimes, the simplest solutions are the hardest to accept. I've found that there's only one way to really avoid drama — be present. In every conversation, be present. In every encounter, be present. In every moment and every word, be present. When you are aware of yourself, it's difficult to run your mouth and later find yourself feeling remorseful about what you should or shouldn't have said.

"If you want to keep a secret, keep it to yourself."

Assume that anything that leaves your mouth is no longer a secret. If it's meant to be confidential, then keep it to yourself. I can't tell you how many times someone has said to me, "This stays between the both of us" only for five other people to repeat the same information to me.

"If someone constantly speaks badly of others to you, it's safe to assume that they will speak badly of you to others."

Maybe you think it's cool; perhaps you think people will like you more... Whatever your reason for engaging a gossip/bad-mouther/sh*t talker, you can be sure that their venom will always make its way back to you. My mom gave me the best advice recently. She said, "Be like the rain. The rain doesn't choose to pour on one person and avoid another. Be kind to all, be compassionate to all, speak well of all. If you can't speak well of someone, then say nothing at all." Keep in mind that this doesn't mean that everyone will appreciate who you are and how you are. What it does mean is that you have chosen to be better, to treat everyone equally and fairly. You have chosen to excuse yourself from the grime and the drama. You have made a choice to rise above it all.

THREE BIG WAYS MEDITATION CHANGED MY LIFE

I strongly believe that if you do not feed your soul, the world will feed it for you. I also believe that if you do not decide who you are, the world will decide for you. I started incorporating meditation into my day because I realized that if I didn't go into each day with a specific intention of what I wanted and needed from that day, I would allow the day to control me instead of taking control of the day. It's interesting that we're constantly thinking about what we feed our bodies. By the end of breakfast, we're already thinking about lunch, dinner, and the snacks we're going to have in between. Feeding our souls, however, barely ever crosses our minds.

This is where meditation comes in. There are so many definitions out there for what it is and what it means. I like to keep things simple—I see it simply as food for my soul.

When I started practicing meditation, my intention was to find inner peace. Not only did I discover that my inner peace was never lost, I found so much more hidden within. Here are three big ways this practice changed my life:

1. It taught me how to forgive

Forgiving others is something that I learned over time. Learning to forgive myself, however, was a whole other beast. You don't realize how harsh you are with yourself until you try meditating and get bombarded with a billion thoughts. *What should I cook tonight? That lady at Trader Joe's was a little nuts. Don't forget to put that check in the mail. What really happened at the end of* Inception? *Is* The Matrix *real? What if Neo took the blue pill* and *the red pill? What is wrong with me? Am I even doing this right? Why can't I stop thinking for a few minutes?*

"Mind is never peaceful; no-mind is peace. Mind itself can never be peaceful, silent. The very nature of the mind is to be tense, to be in confusion. Mind can never be clear, it cannot have clarity, because mind is by nature confusion, cloudiness. Clarity is possible without mind, peace is possible without mind; silence is possible without mind, so never try to attain a silent mind. If you do, from the very beginning you are moving in an

impossible dimension."
—Osho

These days, I don't try to stop the thoughts. I accept that they are there. I observe them as they are. I smile. There's no judgment. It is what it is. And then, there's silence.

2. It taught me to be present

A friend once wrote in a letter to me, "Wherever you go, make sure your heart is where you are." I was 19 years old and I lived primarily in the past and the future, always wishing and hoping for a better moment. Better moments did come, but I was always too busy to fully enjoy them. My head and my heart were already plotting about what could make things even better. Eckhart Tolle wrote in *The Power of Now*, "Nothing has happened in the past; it happened in the Now. Nothing will ever happen in the future; it will happen in the Now."

> "...the past gives you an identity and the future holds the promise of salvation, of fulfillment in whatever form. Both are illusions."
> —Eckhart Tolle, *The Power of Now*

When I meditate, I realize that there is no moment in the future in which I will be perfectly happy and complete. Everything that I need is available to me right in the moment I'm in.

3. It reminds me of who I am

Think of how many times in a day you utter the words "I am." Now think of the words that follow. What I hear so many people say are things such as I am tired, I am fat, I am angry, I am an idiot…the list goes on. What I take from this is that we don't spend enough time with ourselves to really know who we are. If we spent a minimum of five minutes connecting with ourselves daily, there's no way we would think and say such horrible things. Knowing who I am before I step out of my house means no one can project their issues and insecurities on me while I'm out there. My sense of self and self-worth are guarded, protected, and reinforced daily.

> "The student (you, me, all of us) …must stand guard
> more strictly over his thoughts…for every time you say
> 'I am not, I cannot, I have not' you are, whether
> knowingly or unknowingly throttling that great
> presence within you."
> —Dr. Wayne Dyer

There is no right or wrong way to meditate. You can do it anywhere—for 30 seconds or 30 minutes. You don't need to be in lotus position and you don't have to build a special room for it. You don't have to do it every single day, but the more you realize how much value it adds to your life, the more you'll want to do it.

WHAT IF IT ISN'T ABOUT THE BIG PICTURE?

Whenever giving a pep talk, people often say, "It's all about the big picture" or "Keep your eye on the prize." I also often hear, "In the end, you won't remember the hard times." As someone who looks at life as an incredibly intricate puzzle, I can't help but think about how misleading and false these seemingly harmless words of encouragement are. I constantly find myself asking, "What if it really isn't about the big picture?"

If you're a puzzle lover or have ever had the pleasure of working on a puzzle with family or friends, you know that the beginning of putting a puzzle together is the hardest part. That moment when you dump all the pieces on the table is usually one filled with both anxiety and doubt as to how you're going to get the mess in front of you to look like the perfect picture on the box.

In spite of the chaos staring you in the face, you start with one piece. You rummage through the mess and you find other pieces that fit into the first piece. You jam certain pieces together but realize they don't work, so you try again. Depending on how complicated the puzzle is, you may take a breather and come back to it again when you're ready.

Quite often, you find yourself scratching your head and whispering "What? Why? How?" Other times, you get pretty close to pulling your hair out. You search for lost pieces. In fact, it seems like you're always searching for lost pieces. There are times when you almost give up, but you trudge on. When a piece fits into another perfectly, you jump and scream for joy.

Throughout the process of putting the entire puzzle together, you have as many moments of frustration, impatience, and anger as you have elation, joy, and excitement. You realize that every single piece serves a purpose and every single piece holds equal weight; none is greater in value than the other. The piece in the center is just as important as the one on the end. Without each one in place, you end up with a ghastly hole in your perfect picture and so your search for each piece means that much more.

As you put the last piece in and look at your completed work of art, you sigh and appreciate its beauty. What you appreciate more, however, is what it took to create that masterpiece. Every single step of the journey was worth it.

> "One's destination is never a place but
> rather a new way of looking at things."
> —Henry Miller

Life is a beautiful, intricate, and challenging puzzle. Most of the time, it feels like a mess, but there is meaning in the mess. What you'll find at the end of the journey is that although you've reached your destination, it wasn't ever about the destination to begin with. It was all about how you got there. The *how* is what shaped you, molded you, and, in the end, freed you.

You are who you are, ready to take on the next puzzle because of the *how*. So, next time someone tells you that "It's all about the big picture," remember that it's actually about those tiny moments and puzzle pieces. The big picture would be nothing without them.

HOW TO DEAL WITH HEARING
NO

My job requires me to say *no* a lot. As difficult as that is, I also get the opportunity to say *yes* quite often. I think about the people who I say no to and then I think about how many times people say no to me. It always seems a bit harsher being on the receiving end. The interesting thing is that it's never really about the no. It's what you make of it that counts—what you do with it and, most important, what you do after it.

Have you ever been so sure that your life was meant to go in a certain direction, yet when you moved forward to make things happen, all you hit was a dead end? Have you ever pursued a dream that you felt so sure about, yet at every corner you turned, there was a big *no* waiting to smack you in the face?

It's hard to continue pushing forward when your spirit keeps getting crushed. It's certainly incredibly difficult to stand your ground when you are consistently being knocked down.

> "I have not failed seven hundred times. I have not failed once. I have succeeded in proving that those seven hundred ways will not work. When I have eliminated all the ways that will not work, I will find the way that will work."
> — Thomas Edison

I don't think that we ever get accustomed to hearing the word no. It doesn't sting any less the 100th time because you've heard it a hundred times. What I like to focus on is what I've discovered about myself between the first no and the hundredth no. I've learned that hearing no will never take anything away from who I already am, and hearing yes will never add anything to who I already am. Having another person validate or say yes to my dream or vision doesn't make it more real. My dream becomes real the moment I take action. For example, I am a writer because I write, not because someone decided to publish my work.

This concept of self-validation above all other validation can prove difficult in a world where an event isn't real to most people until someone "likes" it on Facebook or Instagram. It's why knowing yourself is the key to the challenge of hearing no. When you know yourself, hearing no isn't immediately tied to your self-worth. No simply means "not here and not now." Your yes is just further down the road. It's not rejection, just redirection.

WHO DO YOU THINK YOU ARE?

"Have I ever told you the story of how the Fox started hunting the Rooster?" my mother asked me last night. "This should be interesting…," I whispered under my breath. In the Yoruba culture (Nigeria), there is not only an adage for every life situation, but there is a folktale for every challenge one faces. I'm grateful for these stories and words of wisdom, as I've heard most of them for most of my life. They're funny, applicable, but, most important, they always teach you something about yourself.

"The Fox didn't always hunt the Rooster. In fact, the Fox was always pretty afraid of this particular bird. He thought that the bright red crest on top of the Rooster's head was live fire. He didn't want to get close as he was afraid of getting burned. The Rooster noticed how the Fox often kept his distance and decided to ask him why. The Fox divulged his fear and the Rooster laughed innocently. 'You don't have to be afraid,' he said. 'It's just extra meat on top of my head. It won't burn you at all.' Relieved, the Fox bid adieu to his feathery new friend. The next time the two creatures met, the Fox felt no fear and approached the Rooster with confidence. He was so comfortable that he grabbed the Rooster crest first and made a nice dinner out of him."

I laughed, but I knew exactly what my mom was getting at by telling me this old folktale. "If you think or say that you're not much, then that is exactly how the world will treat you," she concluded.

A day before our storytelling session, an opportunity had come my way. I wasn't sure if I should say yes. My doubt, surprisingly, wasn't driven by whether or not this opportunity would prove to be successful; my doubt was driven by an annoying voice in my head whispering, "Why me?" It's not the first time I've been asked this question, although it has come more often from other people than from myself.

In addition to recruiting, I have had some great opportunities come my way in the fashion industry. When my extracurricular activities have come up in conversations, a few people have asked, "No offense, but why you? How did they find you? How do you get invitations to events like that?" Not wanting to come off as arrogant, I smile and politely explain that things just worked out the way that they did. As I walk away, my head is screaming, "I've spent many years building my expertise in that field. What do you mean 'why me'? Why not me?"

I've realized that sometimes you have to say these things out loud. It's not arrogance; it's confidence. The fact is that it is not only important for you to know who you are on the inside, but it is also equally important to be able to affirm who you are on the outside. I've often said that if you don't make a decision on what you're worth, the world will decide for you. We coyly show off our "amazing" lives on social media, but if someone compliments us on anything in person, we immediately feel the need to downplay things. When someone says you look great, you respond with "Oh no, I don't look great, look at these bags under my eyes," or maybe a stranger compliments you on what you're wearing, "This is 20 years old," you respond.

We would rather be liked than feared or respected and because of this, we often sell ourselves short. Well, the Rooster sold himself short. He also got eaten for dinner.

WHAT DO YOU KNOW?

"Since the day the late Gene Siskel asked me, 'What do you know for sure?' and I got all flustered and started stuttering and couldn't come up with an answer, I've never stopped asking myself that question."
—Oprah Winfrey

I have always believed that as pursuers of truth and purpose, we go through three stages in this remarkable journey of ours called life. It all begins with "I think"—I think I'm capable; I think I can do this; I think it will be okay…When we begin to grasp the truth behind who we really are, belief steps in. I believe that I can make it; I believe that I'm more than capable; I believe that I can do this. You can think, you can certainly believe, but nothing beats knowing.

When I've found myself in the face of incredibly difficult circumstances, my saving grace has been diving deep into what I know. To know is to trust your journey implicitly. To know is to recognize that there are no mistakes in life. To know is to realize that you are exactly where you are supposed be, doing exactly what you should be doing.

Knowing doesn't mean that doubt won't arise. In fact, the only way to put what you know into practice is to allow doubt to rise up. In knowing, you recognize doubt exactly for what it is —fear or, as I like to call it, fluff. Knowing means accepting what is and surrendering to the present moment. It means seeing a life situation exactly as it is and not the story you've chosen to tell about it. It means letting life flow for you and through you even when you feel like going against the current.

> "People believe themselves to be dependent
> on what happens for their happiness.
> They don't realize that what happens is
> the most unstable thing in the universe."
> —Eckhart Tolle

In happiness and sadness, doubt and confidence, in times of change and periods of uncertainty, what I know has remained my saving grace. Thanks to life's most beautiful and challenging moments, I continue to add to that arsenal. Below are three personal truths that I keep going back to:

1. Nothing and no one can add or take away from who I already am.

2. Nothing ever goes away until it teaches us what we need to know.

3. No challenge or adversity has the power to last forever. It will either end or it will transform.

WHY TRUSTING YOUR INTERNAL GPS IS THE KEY TO YOUR SUCCESS

I used to hate getting lost. The anxiety and uncertainty of not knowing where I was positioned was something that made me very uneasy. When I went somewhere for the first time, I'd research the entire neighborhood. I needed to know if my final destination was to my left or right. Was there parking? Was it on a hill? What were the alternate routes available?

Years ago, when I first started driving in Los Angeles, I purchased a navigation system to help me get around. For some weird reason, however, I would find myself getting paranoid and printing directions before leaving the house to ensure that I was covered in case my GPS went haywire. It was an interesting habit because my experience with the system was that if I took a wrong turn, it would recalculate my route. I always knew when to turn right or left or make a U-turn. Even if it took me the long way home, I still ended up at home. The booming voice from my speakers had never led me astray.

A few days ago, I was on my way back from a glorious adventure at Disneyland. I got off one freeway and hopped on another. It was a route that I was not familiar with, so I was relying heavily on my GPS. I heard the direction to stay left, so I stayed left. Thirty seconds later, I looked up and saw a sign for the 101 freeway all the way to the right. I freaked out. *Shouldn't I be on that side? Why is the GPS silent? Am I lost? I hate being lost.*

I looked to my right as my sister stared at me quizzically. "Did the GPS say anything about taking the 101?" she asked. "No," I responded. "So why are you freaking out?" she said. Thirty seconds later, the voice from my GPS came back on and I was guided to the next exit. In one minute, I had been schooled in the power of faith, trust, silence, and patience—all with the help of one mundane freeway experience.

The voice within, it's there with us every moment of every day. Sometimes, it booms and reverberates through our bodies; other times, it's a bit more quiet—almost like a whisper. Don't go out tonight, take the job, ask for a raise, do it now, wait a little, seize that opportunity, say no… the urgings and guidance go on. Our internal GPS is always there guiding us through the smallest and biggest moments of our lives. You hear the voice when you need it, when it counts. If it's silent, stay the course. Don't go freaking out and jumping on roads you have no business being on.

In our life journey, I believe we have tunnel vision. We can see some of what is in front of us but not all. Our internal GPS, on the other hand, has aerial vision. It's why it's able to calculate the best route for our journeys. I still dislike feeling lost, but I've learned to trust that I'll always find my way home. My internal GPS has never led me astray.

HAPPINESS IS A SKILL.
HERE'S HOW TO MASTER IT

I want a lot of things. Not just physical things. I have goals, dreams, aspirations, and ambitions. I want a lot of things. I rarely judge myself for wanting these things anymore. Once in a while, a thought or two will creep in—demanding that I be content, pleading that I let go of my wants so that I can be less disappointed when they don't happen exactly as I had planned. As soon as those thoughts start to gain momentum, I remind myself that the problem is not with the wanting. The problem is thinking that whatever it is that I want to have will make me happier, more content, or freer.

"People believe themselves to be dependent on what happens for their happiness. They don't realize that

what happens is the most unstable thing in the universe. It changes constantly. They look upon the present moment as either marred by something that has happened and shouldn't have or as deficient because of something that has not happened but should have. And so they miss the deeper perfection that is inherent in life itself, a perfection that lies beyond what is happening or not happening."
— Eckhart Tolle

When I meet the one, get married, have kids, leave this horrendous job, leave this town, get that promotion, buy my dream car, buy my dream house, start my business...then I'll be happy. We tell ourselves these lies in some shape or form throughout our lifetime. Even if you obtained all of the things that you've ever wished for, there will still be one more thing floating around in your head, teasing you and promising your soul completion. The wanting never ends. It's a part of us and there's nothing wrong with it, nor much we can do about it.

Things, money, and people can provide fleeting joy, but long-term happiness is something that can only be discovered and accomplished within the self.

I believe that happiness, like most things worth having, requires some effort on your part. I'm not talking about the kind of happiness where you're jumping, skipping, and screaming with complete and utter joy. Those special moments, when experienced, are so unique and inimitable. They're also impossible to sustain 24/7. The kind of happiness that I'm talking about is that which comes with a "peace that surpasses all understanding" — the kind that already exists within, but which we fail to tap into. Here are a few ways to get back on track:

1. Remind yourself to be happy

This may sound silly because it seems so simple, but the answers to our most baffling questions are usually quite simple. I talk to my mother a lot. We talk about my day, her day, challenges, silly things, and mundane things. There are times when we're talking about difficult situations and I have to remind myself not to get carried away by the emotions swirling around those situations. I feel myself getting sucked in. My voice drops, and so does my energy. In that moment, I hear a gentle reminder, "When was the last time you laughed?" I ease up, let go a little, and allow myself to find some joy in the present moment.

"All negativity is caused by an accumulation of psychological time and denial of the present. Unease, anxiety, tension, stress, worry — all forms of fear — are caused by too much future, and not enough presence.

Guilt, regret, resentment, grievances, sadness, bitterness, and all forms of non-forgiveness are caused by too much past, and not enough presence."

— Eckhart Tolle

2. Be present

How can you be present and have all these dreams, goals, and aspirations? As I mentioned previously, having the dreams, goals, and aspirations isn't the problem. The problem is that we think all of these things will bring us lasting happiness and completion. There is no happiness in the past—that time is already gone, faded to black. There is no happiness in the future—the future doesn't exist. When the future does happen, it will be in the present moment and then the past and then it will also fade to black. Build your dreams, take inspired action, enjoy the process, but don't be tied to a specific outcome and do not depend on that outcome to make you happy.

> "I've set goals. None of them came true. But
> five or six other amazing things that I never
> could have predicted happened instead."
> —Ramit Sethi

3. Be grateful

Gratitude leads to contentment. Contentment allows for freedom. I strongly believe this. Gratitude for the small steps accomplished, the big battles won, the ability to even be in the battle—these are all things that make my soul swell. Whatever the intensity of the challenge you're facing, the moment you step into a place of gratitude, the load lightens up. I believe that gratitude is the language the universe speaks. Tune into it.

> "If peace is really what you want,
> then you will choose peace."
> —Eckhart Tolle

If happiness is really what you want, then you will choose happiness.

IS IT TIME FOR A LIFE AUDIT AND EDIT?

"Edit your life frequently and ruthlessly.
It is your masterpiece after all."
—Nathan W. Morris

I love this quote by personal finance expert, Nathan W. Morris. I must admit, the "ruthless" life edit was something that took getting used to on my part. There's always the fear of what people will think of you. If you cut off a destructive friendship, they'll see you as a horrible person, even as they continue to hurt you. If you say no, you'll be viewed as inflexible. If you choose yourself, you're most definitely selfish. Somehow, you begin to think that it's easier and more convenient to leave things the way they are. You come up with all of these excuses to continue to hold on to garbage and clutter.

I am of the belief that if something doesn't add value to your life, then it doesn't deserve to be in your life. A few times a year, I perform a life audit and follow it with a life edit. I examine my relationships, my work, my passions, and my finances. I take a look at where my energy is going as well as whom and what I'm spending my time on. It's not easy to face the truth when you've been hiding in the shadows.

> "...you are the only person alive who has sole custody of your life. Not just your life at a desk, or your life on the bus, or in the car, or at the computer. Not just the life of your mind, but the life of your heart. Not just your bank account, but your soul."
> —Anna Quindlen,
> *A Short Guide to a Happy Life*

I tell myself often that having a quality life means being thoughtful, observant, and conscious of everything happening around me. Audits and edits are not a onetime thing. You need to frequently make use of them in order to have a quality life.

Whenever I get a chance, I love to watch my mother in her garden. I observe as she cuts and prunes. It looks harsh as she cuts away branches, leaves, and even buds. If you had no idea of the pruning process and were watching this, you'd think there'd be nothing left after. The fact is that you prune to remove the damaged and unproductive parts of the plant. You prune to shape and direct the growth of the plant. You prune to ensure a healthy and blooming plant when its season finally comes.

Letting go of things and people we've become accustomed to is never easy. They could be space fillers, but we refuse to let them go because we're afraid of having an empty space. An empty space is very awkward for a lot of people. The interesting thing about life, however, is that you can't invite something new in until you create the space for it.

IT'S ALL IN YOUR HEAD

When we are young, we are constantly encouraged to use our imagination. Most of us at some point in our childhood made up friends that only we could see. These friends came with very detailed backgrounds and stories. I remember owning a "clothing store" growing up. I was very meticulous about what came in and out of my store. I also perfectly cut up hundreds of pieces of paper to distribute to my family members. This was the money that would be spent at my store. To keep things interesting, I would make up challenging situations that occurred at the store. Maybe someone ran out of money while paying or a customer tried to steal from me. Let's just say there was never a boring moment at chez Wemi.

> "I've had a lot of worries in my life,
> most of which never happened."
> —Mark Twain

When you're a child, drama is a given side effect of an active imagination. When you're an adult, however, too much drama is just a recipe for disaster. This past week, I was expecting a response on a project I'd been working very hard on. I expected to hear back by last Friday. For three days before that, I beat myself up over every possible response and outcome. I thought of every horrible thing that could go wrong. I also thought of the possibility of the great things that could come from this project. I thought about all the work I'd put in and what it would mean if the answer was no.

Friday came and went. I put off checking my e-mail for fear of what was waiting for me. Saturday came and I still hadn't built up the courage to check. I finally took a peek on Saturday evening, and it turns out that my contact was out of town the entire time. There was no dreadful answer waiting for me. I felt so silly. All of that drama and anxiety were for nothing.

> "The primary cause of unhappiness is never the situation but your thoughts about it. Be aware of the thoughts you are thinking. Separate them from the situation, which is always neutral, which always is as it is. There is the situation or the fact, and here are my thoughts about it. Instead of making up stories, stay

> with the facts. For example, 'I am ruined' is a story. It
> limits you and prevents you from taking effective
> action. 'I have 50 cents left in my bank account' is a fact.
> Facing facts is always empowering."
> —Eckhart Tolle

Facing facts is empowering and unless your profession requires it, making up stories about things that may or may not happen will not empower you. The mind is a powerful place. Beautiful things can come from this space of imagination, but so can horrible things. Fears lurk behind our genius. We see their shadows and we assume that they're bigger and more powerful than they actually are.

Sometimes, we can't help but think the worst of a situation. Fear kicks in as our initial reaction and it just spirals out of control from there. A trick that I use is that instead of talking myself out of feeling bad and then feeling even worse for not being able to let go of those thoughts, I let myself sink into that worst-case scenario for a few minutes. I say quietly to myself, if scenario A happens, then B could happen. In spite of this, I will be okay. In that moment, I let go.

There will always be things that are out of our control, people who act and exist outside our field of influence. Accepting this as well as life's moments as they come and as they are is the only way to end our suffering. If you're going to make stuff up, use your powers for good and not evil.

SEVEN THINGS I LEARNED ON MY WAY TO THE TOP OF THE WORLD

The Burj Khalifa is the tallest building in the world. Standing at 2,716.5 feet and housing more than 160 stories, it is truly a sight to behold. I was most recently in Dubai and Abu Dhabi and I knew I couldn't leave the UAE without experiencing life at the top. It turns out that life had a few lessons for me as well.

It is my experience that each hour of each day offers thousands of teachable moments. The question is: Are we watching? Are we listening? Are we paying attention to those moments? When I look back at what life has taught me, I realize that my most profound lessons have always come from the simplest and sometimes mundane scenarios. These seven lessons were no different:

1. Everyone wants to get to the top, but few are willing to pay the cost to get there. There are two levels at which you can enjoy the views at the Burj Khalifa: levels 124 and 148. For some, the view at level 124 is fine, while others want the whole extravaganza. In life and at the Burj Khalifa, you have to ask yourself what you're willing to pay and how far up you want to go.

2. The line and wait time to get to the top is very, very long. Pre-security, I found myself waiting for approximately 30–40 minutes. Getting to the elevator that would take me to the top required another 45 minutes. Any road or journey worth taking will require some wait time to get there. This is when people start giving up. When I was little and would complain to my grandmother about something I couldn't change, she'd say to me, "What cannot be helped must be endured." If you can't change something, then try to endure it. I'll take it one step further and say, try to endure it with a joyful spirit. This is easier said than done, but the only thing that will keep you sane on the way to the top of the Burj Khalifa and your dreams is to try to enjoy yourself while waiting. Make conversation, laugh, observe, and try not to lose yourself to irritation, anger, and anxiety.

3. Be very observant of the people you meet along the way. You learn so much when you watch and observe. What you learn will, in turn, allow you to react consciously to the scenarios unfolding in front of you instead of reacting in fear. From the people who push and shove their way through the line but still end up in the same elevator as you to the little girl sleeping on her mother's shoulder—completely at peace and unaware of the chaos ensuing around her—observe, take it all in. There's always a message within the mess.

4. Be bold and push through, but don't lose yourself in the fight to get to the top. The journey to the top is never breezy. You have to fight your way through and stand up for yourself and what you believe in. It is, however, very easy to get lost in that fight. You start to think only of yourself and how you're going to get where you're going. You do whatever is necessary to get there, becoming selfish and mean with little regard for anyone else. This is why it's important to be equally observant of your inner self as you are with others.

5. You'll get so tired that you'll want to quit. Don't. There's a point while waiting in line for the elevator that you can get a peek of the doors around the corner. There's excitement because you realize that you're so close, but the worst case of fatigue sets in. Physically, your body hurts from the bags and camera you've

been lugging around all day. Mentally, you're drained from all the noise and waiting. You contemplate calling it quits because you're not sure that the view will even be worth it. There's a reason they say that the night is darkest just before dawn. Take one foot, place it in front of the other, and keep moving. That moment will pass.

6. Being at the top may feel differently than you thought it would. When you wait for something for so long, there are always a lot of expectations tied to the end result. This is why it's important to focus less on the destination and more on the journey. So many people fight so hard to get to the top and then they feel empty when they get there. They become frustrated because they thought they'd feel complete. If you weren't complete on your way to the top, you won't be complete when you get there. There are others who get to the top and never stop to be in the moment. They spend so much time posing and taking photos of the experience versus being in the experience. There's nothing wrong with documenting amazing moments—just don't forget to be in it. You've spent so much time waiting for it and wanting it. Make sure you enjoy it.

7. Don't let the experience of getting there make you bitter. Life is filled with millions of Burj Khalifas. It could be starting a new business, starting a family, or

finding your dream job. Keep in mind that the journey to the top of each dream is never exactly the same. Take the lessons you've learned and apply them, but don't ever let the experience of achieving one dream deter you from pursuing another.

THE SCIENCE OF SECOND CHANCES— HOW TO USE YOUR HEAD WITH A LITTLE BIT OF HEART

Character has always been so fascinating to me. Why are people the way that they are? Why do they do the things that they do? I learned pretty early on in life that change is never easy.

A scorpion, being a very poor swimmer, asked a turtle to carry him on his back across a river. "Are you mad?" exclaimed the turtle. "You'll sting me while I'm swimming and I'll drown."

"My dear turtle," laughed the scorpion, "if I were to sting you, you would drown and I would go down with you. Now where is the logic in that?"

"You're right!" cried the turtle. "Hop on!" The scorpion climbed aboard and halfway across the river gave the turtle a mighty sting. As they both sank to the bottom, the turtle resignedly said: "Do you mind if I ask you something? You said there'd be no logic in your stinging me. Why did you do it?"

"It has nothing to do with logic," the drowning scorpion sadly replied. "It's just my character."

Can people change? It is incredibly difficult to change but not impossible. Think about how many times you've dieted and failed, vowed to stop smoking or drinking and failed. Change is a battle and it is not for the faint of heart. It requires strength and, most important, resilience. For most people, change doesn't and cannot happen overnight. You have to be able to pick yourself back up and try again and again and again.

It is also important to note that in spite of how many times you tell a person that she needs to change, she actually has to recognize on her own that there is something that needs changing within her. You can't force someone to seek healing if she doesn't believe she is sick.

Do people deserve second chances? My motto on this is: Be kind, not stupid. If I invited someone into my home and he stole something from me but came back, admitted his wrongdoing and asked for forgiveness, I could forgive him. I could even make him some tea while he sobbed about his transgressions. But I wouldn't leave a Rolex on the table while making tea in the other room. Be quick to forgive, but slow to forget. This doesn't mean holding a grudge, but rather taking a mental note.

Everyone deserves a second chance, but trust must be re-earned. If a client cheats you out of money you've earned, she is dishonest at her core. If you work with her again, she'll do it again. If a coworker throws you under the bus, he will never have your best interest at heart. If a boss undermines you, you will never be able to count on her. If someone constantly speaks badly of others to you, he will speak badly of you to others.

We don't have to dig that deep to discover the true character of others. The truth is never that far from the surface; we just have to pay attention. When someone nonchalantly says to you, "I'm a little selfish" or my favorite, "I'm crazy," don't laugh it off as just words. It's also equally important to pay attention to people's actions. Pay attention to how people treat the waiter/waitress at a restaurant or the way they fight with others—some people fight so dirty that there's no coming back from where they take things.

When contemplating giving someone a second chance, it will invariably come down to the character of the person you're dealing with. Keep in mind that people will always show you who they are; you just have to believe them.

ARE YOU IN DANGER OF LOSING HOPE?

When a baby is hungry, he cries and expects that he will be fed. He doesn't cry and wonder if his mother will hear him. The baby doesn't overthink his actions. He doesn't think or wonder about how his mother will produce the milk he needs, how long it'll take to produce that milk, and when he will be fed. When a baby is hungry, he cries and expects that he will be fed.

We can learn a lot from children: the way they explore, the way they see things with eyes of wonder, and, most important, the authority with which they hope and have faith that anything is possible. Of course, children become adults. They become us and, along the way, adults and life teach them and us to be cautious about hope and faith. We call it being realistic.

We would rather expect that things will go badly than hope that they might turn out well. When a dream doesn't go as planned, we jump at the opportunity to feed our cynicism about life and say, "I knew it wouldn't work." Don't get me wrong; this journey is not the easiest. Whether you're a millionaire or have just one dollar to your name, an employer or employee, married or single, each life path has its own set of challenges and obstacles. Life will take you to the brink and with one tiny miracle, bring you right back. The only way to survive is to remain hope filled.

> "…if you have faith as small as a mustard seed…"
> —Matthew 17:20

There will be times when you feel like you cannot muster any hope. Try and muster just a tiny bit of hope and then try and muster a lot of hope. Remember that an oak tree starts out as an acorn. Hope is light and darkness cannot exist where there is light. Despair cannot exist where there is hope. It's a strange thought, but I think people fear hope. Hope is delicate, powerful, and dangerous. It has the ability to make you feel vulnerable and exposed. We are in danger of looking like fools if things don't work out as planned, so we'd rather protect the ego and settle for less than hope for more. What I've learned is that your success in life will always come down to what you believe. Life isn't out to get you. You are here to learn, grow, build, dream, and live to the fullest of your ability and potential. Life is here to support you every step of the way.

You don't always get what you want in life and that is actually okay. In spite of many ups and downs, desires, and aspirations, I have never tailored my dreams to my reality. I always tailor my reality to my dreams. I expect that, like a baby, when I need something and cry out, the best things in life will always make their way to me. If what I've asked for doesn't make its way to me, then it's not the best for me. Along the way, I continue to hope. It costs me nothing, but it could give me everything.

HOW TO BE A BETTER PERSON TODAY

We spend so much time thinking about the past. We spend a lot more time thinking about the future. If this had only worked out, we think. If this could only work out, we hope. Eventually, time blurs. Our regrets and disappointments of yesterday mix in with our fears and anticipation of tomorrow. Time blurs and we miss out. We miss out on the one thing that actually matters —NOW.

> "Nothing has happened in the past; it happened in the Now. Nothing will ever happen in the future; it will happen in the Now."
> —Eckhart Tolle

1. Be present

I was at a Damien Rice concert a few weeks ago. As I took in the gorgeous view of the Greek Theater in Los Angeles, I watched as so many people rushed in late for the show; I watched as they recorded the entire concert on their phones, their eyes glued to the tiny screens in front of them while completely missing out on the grand and beautiful moment happening just beyond. I watched as they rushed out of the theater before the show was over, missing out on a glorious encore—all so that they could avoid a little traffic on the way out. If we're not careful, we will be a generation that will be remembered for documenting life instead of living it.

> "If you have nothing else to give, give a smile."
> —Yogi Tea

2. Be kind

It's amazing that in this day and age, we're still running around trying to buy our way to being fulfilled. We forget that everything that we really need in this journey has been made available to us completely free of charge. Hope, compassion, kindness, love—they have all been there since the beginning of time. These are the currencies that our world should be running on, but we've decided to write numbers on expertly cut pieces of paper and call them valuable. Be kind to yourself and to others. Hold your tongue when you can; hold your tongue especially when you feel like you can't. Give a smile; give a compliment. Go out of your way, just a little, for someone else. Words are powerful; so are actions. Be compassionate; be kind.

> "I remind myself every morning: Nothing I say this day will teach me anything. So if I'm going to learn, I must do it by listening."
> —Larry King

3. Listen

You're always going to learn more from listening than talking. Even if you don't like what you're hearing, at least you'll be able to make an informed choice for the future from listening in that moment. The fact is that we can all learn a lot from each other. Each of us has a story to tell—a story worth listening to. The problem is that we're all so busy in our self-created bubbles that we don't even realize the amazing connections we're missing out on. When was the last time you actually listened? To your spouse, your coworker, your child? As the other person is talking, we're barely looking at them. All we can think about is what we're going to say next. We are so afraid of pauses and silence that we need to fill them quickly with words. What we forget is that beautiful things happen in moments of silence. For that split second, when you're not trying, you can really hear the person you're talking to. Most important, you can see them.

ARE YOU FLUNKING OUT OF LIFE?

I like to do a nightly check-in with myself. At the end of each day, I run through the events of the day and sit with the pivotal moments that occurred. I don't do this in a judgmental way—although that approach took quite some time to master. The purpose of the exercise is to see where I could have been better at being me. Could I have been more present? Listened more? Been less angry? Was I too sensitive in certain scenarios or a little bit harsh in others? I play everything back, make a few mental notes, and then I let them go. I remind myself that being conscious of the choices I made and continue to make is half the battle. There is always a chance to be better.

You don't stop taking tests just because you're out of school. Life education never stops no matter how many diplomas or certificates you complete and collect. In order to grow you and mature you, life will always test you. You will be tested in every moment of every day. Every action is a test. Every reaction is a test. Some people repeat the same mistakes over and over again. They fail to recognize that they are basically repeating the same test over and over again as well.

> "Insanity is doing the same thing over and
> over again and expecting different results."
> — Albert Einstein

When we fail to recognize the patterns in our lives, we'll find ourselves going around the same circle until we become conscious of the choices leading us around the roundabout. I once realized that I seemed to keep attracting a certain kind of friend over and over again—the kind that bleeds your energy dry and then asks you to give more. It took me years to recognize this pattern. When I did, however, I cleaned house. I made a lot of difficult decisions about my then circle of friends and redefined what true friendship meant to me.

After all this happened, I thought I was done with that chapter, but life had to make sure that I intended to stand by my new promise. The next person that I became friends with was great at first and then the drama followed. How is it possible that I was still attracting the same kind of people with all of my antennas up and my eyes wide open? I knew it was a test and I was determined not to fail. The moment I recognized that this person mirrored my past, I excused myself from the situation. That test has never come up again.

Just like school, in life, if you don't pay attention, you flunk. If you don't study, you flunk. If you don't show up, you flunk. If you find yourself stuck in a situation, look closely at what is happening around you and then look within. What are you supposed to be learning? The same goes for situations that keep repeating themselves. Your *Groundhog Day* won't cease until you pass the test.

> "When I was a child, I spoke as a child, I understood as a child, I thought as a child; but when I became a man, I put away childish things…"
> —1 Corinthians 13:11

There are so many who grow in age but not in wisdom. I blame this on a lack of awareness. Awareness allows you to stop feeling your way through the shadows and lights your path to change. We will never stop being tested. We are here to be the best versions of ourselves and we will be tested until we become that. Pay attention, reflect, be smarter, and be stronger. There is always a chance to be better.

TO FIGHT OR FLOW?

"If you don't fight life, it will take you
where you need to go."
— Keenen Ivory Wayans

There is a rhythm to life — an ebb and flow. It has a beat, even if you can't hear it. That beat is in every plant, every animal, every river, every raindrop, and every human being. It is in every action and reaction; it is in every pause, every word, and every breath. These days, I'm learning more and more about that beat. I've learned that I can either fight it or I can flow with it. In both the best and the worst times of my life, the latter has always been the wiser option.

About a week ago, some incredibly strong winds swept through the city of Los Angeles. They were so strong that many neighborhoods, including mine, lost power overnight. When I woke up that morning, my initial reaction was that of irritation. I had so much to do and very little time to waste. My computer was not at full power, my Internet was out, I couldn't iron, and so forth. It wasn't the first time I had experienced a power outage, although you'd never know that by my reaction. Each time, the impatience, anxiety, and speculation of when I'd finally be able to get on with life would eventually wear me out.

This time around, I recognized that I was in a less-than-ideal situation, but I could decide to react differently. Life has a rhythm and in spite of the chaos around us, that rhythm does not change. The day of the power outage, I chose to step away from my intended schedule. There wasn't much I could do anyway, so I made other plans. As I drove down the street, the traffic lights were out, but the traffic cops were helping by guiding all the drivers through the intersections. I reminded myself that even in chaos, order always exists.

We can't ever forget that there are guides all around us. When all the signals are out, we have to pay attention to those guides and the signs waving us through the intersections of our lives, making sure we don't make the right moves at the wrong times and, most important, making sure that we avoid unnecessary collisions.

I sometimes feel like my entire life is an exercise in the art of patience. I remind myself often that this journey will take however long it'll take and when it comes to my dreams, hopes, and aspirations, I'll get "there" whenever I get "there." Whether we're getting what we want or not in a moment doesn't matter—the time will pass anyway. Being aware of this allows us to choose who we want to be in each moment. On the day of the outage, I treated myself to a massage, ran my errands, and had a lovely lunch. When I got back home, there was light. None of the plans I had earlier mattered at that point.

Life has a rhythm and a beat. There will be different notes that play over that rhythm at any given time. There will be times when we can anticipate which note is coming next. There will be other times when we can't. We need to learn to flow with things. If one plan doesn't work, make another. If you feel you can't make things better, step away from the situation—a solution will eventually reveal itself. Lastly, for those moments that are so dark that I can't see a way through, I make it a point to tell myself that I have never met a night, no matter how long, that didn't eventually give in to the morning.

IS IT WORTH YOUR PEACE?

"If it is peace you really want,
then you will choose peace."
—Eckhart Tolle

I always come back to these words. When I'm anxious or irritated, perplexed, frustrated, annoyed, impatient, unsure, angry, or unhappy, I always come back to these words. No matter how powerless I feel in a situation, I never stop thinking that I have a choice. There are so many things that we can't control in life, and yet there is one thing we can always control and that is how we react to whatever life or people throw at us.

"Is that so?"

Eckhart Tolle tells a story in his book *A New Earth* about the well-respected Zen Master Hakuin, who lived in a small town in Japan. The teenage daughter of his next-door neighbor became pregnant and while being questioned by her angry parents as to the identity of the father of her child, she pointed the finger at Hakuin. Her parents angrily confronted him, telling him that their daughter had confessed to him being the father of her unborn child. "Is that so?" was all the monk would say.

Word spread and the Zen Master lost his reputation and a lot more. When the child was born, the parents demanded he take the child into his care because it was his responsibility. He responded again, "Is that so?" A year later, the teenager remorsefully confessed to her parents that the real father of the child was the young man who worked at the butcher shop. Her parents, feeling guilty, went to apologize to the monk and ask for forgiveness. "We are really sorry. We have come to take the baby back. Our daughter confessed that you are not the father." "Is that so?" is all the Zen Master would say as he returned the child to the family.

Wouldn't it be amazing if we could all tap into a place where nothing could disturb our peace? Wouldn't it be absolutely life changing if we could be that stream where no matter how many surface ripples are caused by people throwing pebbles at us, we still remain calm at our core? It may be easier said than done, but it isn't impossible.

What is so important to have the power to make you un-happy? Is that annoying coworker really worth your peace? Is the guy who cut you off in traffic worth your peace? Whenever I find myself in a potential "peace stealing" moment, I do three things:

1. I take the soap bubble test

I put whatever problems cornering me at the moment in individual soap bubbles and then I ask myself, if I got scary news about a death, accident, or illness in that moment, would the bubbles stand? Of course not. They would dissipate into thin air. It's important to be aware that we are always going to be surrounded by soap bubble moments. We experience so many trivial "problems" that don't really matter in the grand scheme of things.

2. I resist the urge to fight back

Whenever someone does something that hurts us, our ego gets dinged. We think they've taken something from us and we have to fight in order to get it back. News flash: No one can take or add anything to who you already are. Don't get me wrong: This isn't a permission slip to become a doormat. There are times when you have to stop the party to speak your truth. The difference between that truth versus a revenge of words is in how much awareness you're carrying in you. For a split second, it might make you feel better to show them who is boss, but, again, your reaction doesn't really mean much in the grand scheme of things. Your perception of loss is an illusion.

You don't gain anything by going after someone who hurt you because you never truly lost anything to begin with.

3. I choose how I react

Deep inside, I know what's right. I know what matters and what doesn't, and I know that nothing is worth giving up my peace for. Most important, I know that nothing and no one can make me feel less than I am unless I let them. In spite of this knowledge, I still sometimes allow certain life situations to get the better of me. I try not to be too hard on myself when this happens. It's preparation for the next time. It's a path taken that doesn't have to be taken again. Although it can be exhausting being a watcher of my actions, I recognize that the more conscious I am, the more aware I am of the power of my choices. It's really easy in the end, if it's peace that I really want, then I will always choose peace.

STILL WAITING?

"Life is made up of moments, small pieces of
glittering mica in a long stretch of gray cement.
It would be wonderful if they came to us
unsummoned, but particularly in lives as busy as
the ones most of us lead now, that won't happen.
We have to teach ourselves how to live, really live...
to love the journey, not the destination."
— Anna Quindlen, *A Short Guide to a Happy Life*

They say life is what happens when you're
busy making other plans, but I say life is
what happens when you're waiting for life to happen. So
many of us spend so much time waiting on a better moment
than the one we're in. We've convinced ourselves that we'll
finally be happy when that moment arrives. We wait for our
lives to start and tell ourselves that things will be better when

we have a new job, take a vacation, get married, have kids, buy a house, get divorced, save up the perfect amount of money to travel... the list goes on.

Nothing is ever perfect. If there is one thing life guarantees us, it's that we will always face challenges. There will never be a time when everything is absolutely perfect. Talk to a famous actor, athlete, or musician, and they'll never say that they have the perfect life. They do everything that they can to "make it" and then realize that "making it" comes with its own set of problems. From higher taxes to fake friends, loss of privacy, and intense public scrutiny, even the strongest characters find it difficult to adjust.

> "Life will give you whatever experience is most helpful
> for the evolution of your consciousness. How do you
> know this is the experience you need? Because this is
> the experience you are having at the moment."
> —Eckhart Tolle

You are here, now, having this experience because this is what you need. Don't fight it, don't ridicule it, and don't diminish it. If you resist it, it will persist. If you ignore it, it will linger until you acknowledge it. If you choose to completely remove yourself from the moment and wait for a better one, it will return in another shape or form until you learn what you were meant to learn in the first place.

No past or future moment will bring you lasting happiness. No two moments are the same. If you miss what you have now, it can never be exactly as it was. There are so many beautiful moments happening in the midst of our journey, whether we choose to acknowledge them or not. I used to wait for the big moments; I've gotten better at just being in those moments — whether big or small.

> "Wherever you are, be there totally. If you find your here and now intolerable and it makes you unhappy, you have three options: remove yourself from the situation, change it or accept it totally."
> — Eckhart Tolle

The routine of talking to my little sister via Facetime before bed every night brings me such bliss. So does listening to jazz on a Friday night in a half-empty restaurant. The smell of fresh bread always brings a smile to my face, so does the first whiff of autumn. I have felt no stronger feeling of calm and happiness as when I stroll down the streets of Paris after dinner or watch the sunset by the river Seine.

Today, as I put together my weekly flower arrangements for my apartment, there was a moment when I realized that I needed nothing else than what I had in that moment. Not only that, but everything that I was doing, seeing, and feeling in that moment counted for something. Every petal, every bud, and every sound of a breaking branch—it all mattered. This was it. There was nothing more to wait for.

WHAT DO YOU SEE?

I recently heard about a woman who had an animal dash into her home unexpectedly. She thought it was a donkey and quickly grabbed a broom to scare off the animal. Shortly after the animal entered her home, a few zoo officials stormed in, asking if she'd seen anything. She said a donkey just dashed in and that she'd been trying to beat it out of hiding. The officials immediately ushered her out, while letting her know that it was actually a recently escaped lion paying her a visit.

"Perception is reality."

Maybe she didn't have her glasses on, but I love this lady's spunk in grabbing a broom to beat her intruder out of hiding and, essentially, out of her home. She perceived the lion to be a donkey and treated the animal as such. There was no fear, just a feeling of annoyance. The moment the people around her mentioned that it was a lion, however, everything changed. What she perceived to be small immediately grew 5000 times bigger.

There are the things that are happening around us and then there's the way we regard, understand, and interpret the things happening around us. There is reality and then there's the story we tell about reality. You are an unattached woman; that could be your reality. You are hopelessly single, with no foreseeable prospects, and you're probably going to die alone —that is the story you've concocted around your reality. You have $50 in your bank account; that could be your reality. You are poor, destitute, and will end up homeless with no friends and future if nothing changes immediately—that is the story your ego has made up around your life situation.

"I am the greatest, I said that even before I knew I was."
—Muhammad Ali

There is magic in knowing who you are—who you truly are. Sometimes, you have to keep saying things until your belief catches up to your words. But, when you know who you are, your perception of things will always slant toward that truth. Keep in mind that whenever your ego has a chance to choose between what is and the story of what is, it will always choose the latter. It finds comfort in the latter. The latter is where it finds its identity—away from who you truly are.

"Some historians hold that history… is
just one damned thing after another."
— Arnold Toynbee

How do you see life? How do you see yourself? Do you perceive your life as just "one damned thing after another"? Do you see yourself as a pawn in life's cruel game? Do you see yourself as powerless to life's circumstances? Often, during a transaction, a seller will say to a buyer, "what you see is what you get." I think this applies to life as well. What you see and perceive about life is exactly what you can expect to get out of life.

You are not a victim of your reality or circumstance. You are not powerless and you are not weak. Life is not here to chew you up and spit you out, and whatever your life situation is at the moment, remember that "all is creation, all is change, all is flux, all is metamorphosis" (Henry Miller,1944).

Know this truth, see this truth, and then watch this truth set you free.

FINDING BEAUTY IN THE SPACE

I can't explain it. In fact, trying to put it into words diminishes the entire experience. It's not the first time that I've felt this; I'm sure I've felt it many times before. It seems to me that it exists with and without my permission at least a million times a day. It flees, it stays, but mostly it flees. I breathed in the breeze as I stood in front of the mirror; it seemed to pass through me and over me all at the same time. The light was just light enough; the air was just warm enough. My heart fluttered a little and I wasn't sure why. There was a familiarity to this space, but then there was a fear of what I might discover.

I forgot where I was and what I was supposed to do next. I forgot myself, my dreams, my goals, my ambitions, and my aspirations. I forgot that everything that was supposed to be done this weekend was actually not done. I forgot to be hard on myself; I forgot to forgive myself. I forgot every physical ache and emotional dent. In that moment, in that space, nothing was being asked of me, yet I was being given everything that I needed. In that moment, I experienced a peace that surpassed my understanding. I discovered a place of no mind, a gap… it was perfect.

> "I think, at a child's birth, if a mother could ask a fairy godmother to endow it with the most useful gift, that gift should be curiosity."
> —Eleanor Roosevelt

I was always a curious child, so it makes sense that I grew into a very curious adult. Curiosity is fantastic, but when the need to know turns into an obsessive need to always know what comes next, curiosity becomes a detriment to the human spirit. It's amazing to me that so many people will never experience that first nervous phone call with the person who they just gave their number to—the person they locked eyes with and instantly connected with. The person they hoped would call and who is now on the other line.

They'll never experience the fear of thinking that the other person can hear their heart beating through the phone. They'll never experience the awkward pauses and gaps in conversation and not knowing what the other person is going to say next. So many of us will never experience this feeling because so many of us are afraid of those gaps and pauses. We'd rather text. It's easier to plan and anticipate when we text—there is less room for surprises, which means there's less room for magic. How sad.

"We plan...God laughs."

There is beauty in not knowing what comes next—whether it's a moment of no thought—of no mind—or a period in your life when you have absolutely no clue about what to do and no idea of what will happen. If you take a minute to rest in that space, to still your mind and your preconceived ideas of what should be, if you take a minute to be in that moment and not run away into the possibilities of the future, you are bound to find awe in that unplanned gap.

"Accept the present moment and find the perfection that is untouched by time."
—Eckhart Tolle

The gap is a moment of perfection between what is and what isn't. It lives and operates in a place and space that is beyond our thoughts, human manipulations, and even sometimes comprehension. We're usually afraid of it because it seems so foreign yet so familiar—it is the key to our truest self. Did you know that human beings—and in fact all physical things in general—are made up of nothing? The atoms that make up our bodies are mostly empty space. It is that same empty space that binds and separates the bodies of water on this Earth and beyond. It is that empty space that fills the skies and supports the sun and the moon. It is because of that empty space, that nothingness, that we are actually something.

I find it interesting that the word "nowhere" is also "now here." The next time you want to run away from a place and space of nothing, please stop and stay. You know that space; you are that space. No "bad" thing can come from that space. To trust, to live, and to breathe that unknown space shows that you trust in life itself. Remember that from nothing comes everything.

THE DANGER IN TRYING TO KEEP UP

Who are you trying to keep up with these days? In the early to mid-2000s, I remember watching shows such as MTV's *Cribs* and VH1's *The Fabulous Life of...* I recall the endless lists of things, services, and places that the featured celebrities apparently had access to. Every single episode was designed to fuel judgment on your self-worth. These people were living a much bigger and much more privileged life than you. In essence, their lives were better than yours.

"No one can make you feel inferior
without your permission."
—Eleanor Roosevelt

These days, you don't need flashy magazines and absurd television programs to show you the many ways in which your life doesn't measure up to others. You have Facebook, Instagram, and Snapchat for that. Gone are the days of graduating from high school or college and never giving a second thought to the people who added little or no value to your life. Now, you're Facebook friends. You don't have real conversations with them; your profiles and feeds are just there as reminders of how much better or worse your lives are in relation to the other person.

"#Goals #RelationshipGoals #SquadGoals #LifeGoals"

Worshiping, idolizing, and comparing other people's lives to our own—that is the reality these days. It's as prevalent in groups of 13-year-old girls as it is in groups of 40-year-old men. News flash: There will always be someone more beautiful, skinnier, richer, taller, or smarter than you. Show me the person who has everything, and I'll find you someone who has just a little bit more than that person.

> "Statistically, the probability of any one of
> us being here is so small that you'd think
> the mere fact of existing would keep us all
> in a contented dazzlement of surprise."
> — Lewis Thomas

It is an insult to who you are at your core to think that you are in any way, shape, or form less than anyone else out there. Your journey is individual and unique and nothing about it is an accident. The sooner you realize this, the sooner you can start to embrace the magic brewing underneath every piece of your life puzzle.

> "Comparison is the thief of joy."
> —Theodore Roosevelt

The fact is that we all live curated lives online and even sometimes offline. No one really shares every single thing that is happening in their real lives without some sort of filter over it. I remember a photographer friend mentioning to me that when he first started building his portfolio, he would reach out to potential models via social media. He found it quite odd that some models would ask him for a ride to the shooting location. After all, these were girls who were posing in thousand-dollar clothes and accessories online, but their reality clearly didn't reflect their filtered social media lives.

There is no perfect life out there. A lot of us are just doing the best that we can with what we have. Be brave, look forward, and run your race to the best of your ability. There is no one else who can run that race—and that is precisely why you were chosen to do it.

I AM A LITTLE EMBARRASSED TO ADMIT THIS, BUT...

I worry. Still. Even after all that I know, even after all that I've experienced, and after the many ways that life has proven to me that I need not be anxious about anything—even after all this, I still sometimes allow worry to creep up and make a nice, comfy spot to rest in my head. When a problem arises, I worry that I won't find the right solution. When I take on a new opportunity, I worry about how well it will fit into my future. I worry that I'll run out of things to write about. I worry a lot about wasting time—wasting time on the wrong passions, people, and experiences.

"The mind is a superb instrument if used rightly.
Used wrongly, however, it becomes very destructive.

To put it more accurately… you usually
don't use it at all. It uses you."
—Eckhart Tolle

The mind is a funny thing. I've discovered that it loves to chew on whatever it can get its hands on—it doesn't matter how big or small the circumstance or problem is. We tell ourselves often that when we get the things that we want, we'll finally be happy, content, and at peace. The fact is that even if you got every single thing you've ever wanted, your mind would still find something else to focus on, something else to chew on and fight for and mull over. Worry will eventually ensue about what comes next and how you will achieve that next thing. I've learned that while the mind can be helpful in so many ways, while it can create the most beautiful and magical things, it can also be dangerous if you're not conscious of how it works.

Each of our journeys is a collaboration between us and life itself. If we trust in life, if we believe that we are not here by accident but so that life can know itself in all its glory, then how could we ever be worried about any step of the journey? It is said that the human heart beats about 100,000 times in one day and about 35 million times in a year. During an average lifetime, it will beat more than 2.5 billion times. I do not have to remind my heart to beat. I assume that it will do so without my worrying, nudging, or negotiating. I trust that it will do what it was created to do. What I am discovering is that if I trust in life and in my journey, then I have absolutely nothing to worry about.

"Boredom, anger, sadness, or fear are not 'yours,' not personal. They are conditions of the human mind. They come and go. Nothing that comes and goes is you."
— Eckhart Tolle

I've found that worry is something that sneaks up when the mind is bored. It is afraid of the silence and the consciousness that surrounds it. Just as darkness cannot fully exist in the presence of the tiniest flicker of light, worry and anxiety cannot exist in the presence of consciousness and the now. I have become a watcher of my thoughts. I watch with no judgment. The worries still come, but like an owner watches her dog chase its own tail, I watch with amusement as my mind chases problems it has deemed important. I watch and I wait, and, eventually, the mind tires of its own games. Peace comes. Finally.

THE ART AND ACT OF SURRENDER

"What could be more insane than to oppose
life itself, which is now and always now?"
— Eckhart Tolle

I've often struggled with the word *surren-der* as well as the many meanings it holds. From "yielding power or control" to "ceasing resistance," I've realized that there is definitely an art to living a life of surrender. Even as I type these words, I am aware of the fact that my mind flinches each time I type *surrender*. As someone who believes in fighting for what I want and never giving up, it is hard to come to terms with the idea of yielding my power to another.

"Surrendering to life is the end of suffering."

We are incredibly intelligent beings, but, sometimes, that intelligence can work against us. The same mind that creates and brings magical ideas to life can also harbor pain, anxiety, stress, and worry. What I've realized is that surrender is a matter of perception. If your mind believes that it's giving up power or control, it will fight to hold on to both. However, if it believes that it is allowing what is, to be, then there is no fight against the inevitable.

Surrendering to life is not about submission to a force that you have no control over. Life, whether we believe it or not, is not a separate entity from us. The same energy that runs through every "thing" from the rivers to the birds of the air to the sands at sea to the air we breathe is the same energy that runs through us. It is impossible to break that bond. I think about adding a drop of water to the sea and then trying to take back that same drop from the sea. It would be impossible to do so as that drop was always a part of that sea whether it was separate or together.

When we fight life, life fights us back. I know this for a fact. I also know that some of the best things that have ever happened in my life have happened without my "help." It is not about giving up but, instead, allowing your intuition to lead you toward inspired action. You are not fretting or worrying or chasing and you are not tied to any particular result or outcome—you are acting from a place of truth and trust.

"Surrender to what is. Say 'yes' to life — and see how
life suddenly starts working for you rather than
against you."
— Eckhart Tolle

I'm not advocating a lazy life, but I am advocating trusting life. I strongly believe that whatever is happening at any given moment is happening for a reason. Be alert: There are always valuable lessons to be learned. Surrender is not about not living. In fact, when you surrender is when true living actually starts.

THE END OF SUFFERING

"Why do anxiety, stress, or negativity arise? Because
you turned away from the present moment. And why
did you do that? You thought something else was
more important. One small error, one misperception,
creates a world of suffering."
— Eckhart Tolle

I had been fidgeting for the past five minutes and couldn't figure out what was
wrong. I didn't have to be anywhere, I had no immediate
deadlines, and yet my mind was darting back and forth. There
had to be something I was missing... but I knew there was
nothing missing because I have watched my mind long enough
to know when it is repeating a pattern and it repeats patterns
quite often.

Studies have shown that most of our thoughts are repetitive. It's actually rare that we have new thoughts. Instead, most of us dance between the past and the future, repeating the same conditioned patterns of thinking. This loop plays over and over through the day. When a new day starts, we do the same thing again.

The mind is a beautiful thing and it is indeed "a terrible thing to waste." It can solve the most complex problems, but what it actually ends up doing is chewing on the same thoughts over and over. We have relinquished control to the mind; we allow it to continuously search for and create problems because we are afraid of what we might find in ourselves — outside of the patterns we've created and have embedded in our souls.

We are the creators of our own suffering. If each of us had a billion dollars in the bank, perfect homes and marriages, perfect children — if we all had perfect lives — we would still find a way to deny the present moment. Our minds would still find ways to create drama. Because if there was no drama, what would we do with the silence? The stillness? The world is filled with challenges, but we seem to be the only creatures who think that we can deny what is, fight against nature and her current, and actually win.

Nature does not know good or bad. She only knows what is. When a storm comes and bends a palm tree to the point where its head actually touches the ground, there is acceptance that the storm is present. The tree may stand firm at first, it may sway, and it may stay bent for some time. After the storm, it springs back up.

"Whatever is happening, is happening for a reason…"

The funny thing is that whatever is actually happening in the present moment is rarely ever the problem. What rules is fear —fear of loss, sadness, solitude, and emptiness. So, if enlightenment is the end of suffering, the acceptance of what is as it is, then embracing the present moment is the only way out. Life is transient; it is flux. What is, is what is. It might change and it might not, but, most likely, it will.

FEELING IS BELIEVING

"A man's character may be learned from the adjectives
which he habitually uses in conversation."
— Mark Twain

I was once having snacks with a friend. We sat, chatted, and laughed, and I asked if I could have some almonds from his plate. He jokingly responded, "I'm not really the sharing type." I sensed that he was actually being honest. Another time, I was speaking to the same friend about something that I don't recall the specifics of. What I do recall is that he mentioned jokingly that he didn't really "play well with others in the sandbox." Again, I had a feeling that he was right. My grandmother used to say that underneath every joke is an ounce of truth. I believe that underneath every word uttered is an ounce of a person's true character.

Some people try very hard to hide who they truly are from others, but most people are easily readable or, as I prefer to say, "sense-able." There are people you meet and immediately feel a connection with and then there are others with whom no matter how much you try, you can't seem to shake the feeling of disconnectedness. Do not ignore this feeling. One important life lesson I've been lucky to experience is that it's never really about what I think of the people I meet; it is, however, always about how I feel. So far, my feelings haven't led me astray.

Words and actions reflect different elements of what's happening both on the conscious and subconscious levels of a person's psyche, but there is a deeper level of intuition and feeling that most people don't even tap into. Why is it that a bride will still go through with a wedding even as she feels a horrible sense of dread and doom on the day that is supposed to be the happiest day of her life? Why is it that people go through with business deals even when they sense that they're making a huge mistake?

When someone tells you that he's broken, incapable of love, selfish, or that he gets angry easily, please believe him. When you sense that a job opportunity isn't what it seems to be, please trust your gut. When someone tells you that she can't give you what you're looking for, please say thank you and walk in the other direction. When you sense that someone has no honor or integrity, it is your responsibility to give credence to that feeling. You don't recognize that feeling of doubt and choose to continue. You don't make excuses for people or about the situation, and you definitely don't retreat into a state of denial.

"There is a voice that doesn't use words. Listen."

—Rumi

Common sense and intuition are two of the greatest gifts ever given to mankind. They are like muscles: The more you use them, the stronger they become. We are often reminded to use our heads, but in focusing so much on our thoughts, we ignore how we feel. Our ability to sense and to know from a place that isn't touched by the mind is truly a phenomenal potential, but it will remain a potential unless we tap into it and allow it to work for us.

HOW TO EMBRACE CHANGE

I love autumn. I love the period of transition because it forces me to stop and acknowledge change. I love that it helps me see beauty in the things that I take for granted. I love that I feel romantic, melancholic, and happy all at the same time. I love the changing and falling leaves; I love the gray and cloudy skies. I love the beautiful music, poems, books, and creative energy that always seem to find me during this season. I love that there always seems to be a little spice in the air. I woke up this morning to that change happening again along with butterflies in my stomach.

I didn't always embrace change so willingly. I've fought it, argued with it, negotiated with it, and tried to plead my way out of it. I learned quickly that the only way out is acceptance. Change is scary, whether it's moving into a new job or higher position, having your first child, or leaving a relationship. There are also the kinds of changes that we choose and those that choose us. Either way, the path to freedom is the same — you must embrace change with all that you are.

"...if a hare has seven skins, a man may skin himself seventy times seven times without being able to say, 'Now that is truly you; that is no longer your outside.'"
— Friedrich Nietzsche

Change, like most of life's challenges, is meant to skin you, to build you and forge you, to make way for the best of you. I remember moving to the United States when I was 13. Despite leaving my home and friends, I was incredibly excited for a new experience. I had grown up listening to my parents' stories about traveling the world and this was my chance to build my story. What I didn't anticipate was that a bunch of ignorant kids would drive me into becoming a shell of myself. About two years into my journey, I realized that the girl who went after what she wanted with confidence and vigor had become quiet and fearful of everything.

All I did was look. I stopped participating and became a full-time observer of life. It would take another few years before I found my voice again. After growing out of that stage, I would often get angry with myself for letting people get to me the way that they did. These days, I see that period of my adolescence as life changing. Most of the insight that I have about why people are the way they are and, most important, why I am the way that I am, came to me during those quiet years. I wouldn't change those experiences if I could.

> "What you resist persists."
> — Carl Jung

It's normal to want to push back at what you don't fully understand. When you don't know what's waiting for you on the other side, fear takes over and your mind starts building all kinds of crazy stories about the future. Ninety-nine percent of the time, those stories will not come to fruition. If by any chance they do, it is not the end of the world. You adapt and you figure it out.

There's only one way that I know how to embrace change. It is with open arms, with grace, with acceptance, and, most important, with the knowledge that whatever circumstance or life situation I'm facing is eventually bound to change.

TEN THINGS BEYONCÉ TAUGHT ME ABOUT LIFE

"See the end..."

I've always believed that life has a very interesting sense of humor. It also has many lessons to teach. To the constant seer, hearer, and doer, there's a lesson followed by a wink around every corner. I can almost hear life whispering, "Did you hear that?" ... "Did you see that?" ... "Did you get that?" ... "Remember that." There are lessons in watching nature, animals, and people just like there are lessons in attempting to get last-minute tickets to a sold-out Beyoncé concert.

I decided that I was going to attend the Beyoncé concert at Dodger Stadium months in advance. I've never been part of the "Beyhive," but from watching a few of her concert documentaries and getting firsthand accounts from friends who had attended previous concerts, I knew it would be a great show. The plan was to buy tickets as soon as they went on sale, but I made some new friends over the summer who convinced me that we could get killer tickets at the last minute for a fraction of the cost. The trick was to wait till the very last minute—sounds like a fantastic plan, right? Unfortunately, concert day rolled around, ticket prices kept rising, and I was left contemplating whether to buy nosebleed section tickets for close to $200, continue to wait for a miracle, or call the whole thing off.

Lesson #1
Life does not like wishy-washy

Ask for what you want and be clear about your exact desire. Should I go? Should I not go? But I love *Lemonade* (both the album and the drink)…Maybe I'm not meant to go…The more chaotic things got in my head, the more chaotic things were in real life. My friend and I found a pair of tickets, but then they were purchased right out from under us. We found another pair, but the prices suddenly went up. I realized that I needed to make up my mind. I finally made a commitment to go and set a price limit for the ticket that I wanted. The moment I became clear about what I wanted, the wheels started turning in my favor.

Lesson #2

Trust that you will receive the answer for what you want and that it will be the best possible scenario

At around 4:30 p.m., I still had no tickets, but I got word from my friend that some new tickets had been released at the box office. Another friend of ours was now rushing there to buy those tickets. We later found out that they were Dugout seats for a little over $200, but there was no guarantee that we would get them. The anxiety and tension that followed was absolutely ridiculous. Now I really wanted to go. When you want something so badly that it mentally hurts to think about not having it, it's time to let go and trust. I do a little exercise of "seeing the end." I imagine myself having what I want. The trick is not only visualizing, but also feeling the end result as if it is already happening. In my case, I saw my friend texting me a confirmation of the tickets. I knew I would squeal when that happened, so I saw and felt that squeal in my mind's eye. I saw myself dancing and singing along at the concert. I could feel the bass running through my veins. My feet were itching to dance. I trusted and I saw the end.

Lesson #3

Ignore the naysayers

There are always going to be people who don't believe in your dream, such is the nature of most human beings. You have to learn to ignore these people. There were a lot of people jokingly telling me that there was no possible way that I was going to that concert and that I should have bought tickets ahead of time. Maybe they were right, maybe not. In that moment, it was important to tune out the noise and keep my eye on the prize.

Lesson #4
Prepare for what's coming and fake it till you make it

While waiting to hear if we got the tickets, I had two options. I could either wait in anxiety or prepare to receive what I'd asked for. In this case, I could sit in the office and wait for an answer or go home and get ready.

Lesson #5
Pay attention to the signs

As I drove home to get ready, a car popped up in front of me with the license place "DIVA434." To anyone else, it would have meant absolutely nothing, but to my expectant mind, it was a sign—a wink to lift my spirits. Sometimes, all you really need is faith the size of a mustard seed—just a little hope to carry you through to the finish line. Don't discount the signs, no matter how small or silly they may seem to the cynical mind.

Lesson #6
Take a leap of faith. Go all in or not at all

I got home and freshened up my makeup while still waiting for confirmation of the tickets. The only thing left to do was put on my lipstick. I held off because I thought about the process and annoyance of having to wipe it off if everything fell through. As silly as it sounds, I could sense inside me that this was a sign that I still wasn't fully convinced that I'd be able to go. I recognized this and decided to put the lipstick on. The moment I did, I received a text message from my friend letting me know that we were able to secure the tickets. We were going to see Beyoncé! When you go all in, you are signaling to the universe that you have nothing to lose. It can be a scary thing to jump without a safety net, but it is more scary to not jump at all.

Lesson #7
Be present

It always comes down to this, doesn't it? After all of those suspense-filled hours waiting to find and confirm those tickets, more hours waiting in traffic to get to the venue, and, finally, making it to our seats in the middle of the first song, we pulled out our phones and started recording. It makes no sense to want and wait and finally get what you want just to allow what you've strived so hard for to pass you by. Thankfully, my phone died midway through the fourth song. The fact is that if I wanted to watch Beyoncé on a screen, I should have stayed home and watched YouTube. We live in a world where most of us would rather experience a staged life than a lived life. It takes work to remind the self to just be, but it is work that is well worth it.

Lesson #8

Life is more interesting with twists and turns

It's not easy dealing with uncertainty, but the best stories I've ever been told and the best ones I've ever had the pleasure of reading were filled with intrigue, ups and downs, and suspense-filled moments. I think about all the drama that led to a night of amazing performances and one of the best times I've had in a long time, and I smile at how the twists and turns made for a better narrative. Life is equally filled with nail-biting and unpredictable moments. Those moments are what make it worthwhile.

Lesson #9

You, too, can do what you love and get paid for it

In the middle of the show, Beyoncé mentioned how she'd been doing what she loved since she was 15 years old. I marveled as the audience cheered and screamed her name. She stood in the spotlight in her 5' 7" glory and I thought to myself, "she has two eyes, two ears, two legs, and one voice. She's not from another planet and she doesn't have superhuman strength. She has a gift and she has used that gift to forge a path for herself." The beautiful thing is that we are all gifted with what life saw fit for us to have. How we develop those gifts is up to us. What I saw as this artist #slayed on stage is that with hard work, dedication, and perseverance, nothing is ever truly out of reach.

Lesson #10
Exceedingly and abundantly above what you desire

I started this article with "seeing the end." The end that I saw was what I got, but what I got was even more than I bargained for. My friend and I actually ended up paying less than the quoted price of the tickets, and we also got some fantastic Dugout seats. Our $30 parking fee was waived because the show had to start and the parking attendants were waving all the late attendees through. We found the perfect parking spot right in front of the main entrance to the stadium, and it took us less than 15 minutes to get out of the stadium and onto the freeway after the show (a rare feat).

Trust, clarity, perseverance, and presence—all major lessons learned from a minor life experience. Like I said, life has a very interesting sense of humor.

REALITY CHECK: ARE YOU GROWING OR STAGNANT?

With every new season comes new hopes, dreams, desires, and resolutions. The excitement of starting afresh courses through us like adrenaline, promising one thing—change. For most people, the adrenaline will eventually simmer. Old habits, thoughts, and doubts ultimately creep back in, offering the comfort of the life we're used to. Sooner or later, we succumb to the old and the possibility of change remains just that—a possibility.

> "If you do not change direction, you
> may end up where you're heading."
> —Lao Tzu

As little children, most of us probably had the experience of having our parents track our growth against a wall at home. For each new inch, another mark was added, followed by a proud smile. As adults, there are things that we believe are obvious signs of growth, such as graduating from high school, going to college, getting a job, getting married, or having kids. Although these are all wonderful milestones, they're not necessarily the best growth quantifiers. I say this because despite many adults going through the aforementioned phases, many are still as confused and miserable as ever.

So, how do we know we're growing? I believe the answer lies in how much trust we have in life itself. Life is never going to exist in a straight line—the beauty is in its curves. I find that a true test of growth is how we react and respond to those expected and unexpected curves over time. If we are growing in age and stature, but remain the same internally, can we truly claim growth? If we get just as angry, frustrated, and fearful of every life situation at 40 years of age as we did at 19 years of age, can we really claim growth? If every time we encounter a problem, we panic, believing that we'll never survive it, can we look in the mirror and be proud of whom we've become?

"I've been here before..."

I've recently found myself repeating these words. No, I'm not a time traveler, but I recognize that certain life challenges do often repeat themselves. They may present in different forms, but the core remains the same. If I've been there before, then I don't have to go down the same path—I can change and, most important, I can grow. Choosing the unbeaten path is never easy. You have to battle against fear and doubt, but when you dare to venture into the unknown and trust that life will support you in the process, you can proudly stand up against the measurement wall in your mind and mark another inch above your head.

I've often said that I believe that we grow through three different stages in this human experience: thinking, believing, and knowing. I think I can be great versus I believe I can be great versus I know I can be great. When you get to the stage of knowing, you are now working in collaboration with life instead of trying to fight the flow. Keep in mind that the level of trust that is required to exist in a place of knowing calls for huge growth and that growth doesn't happen overnight. When things are really tough, I like to focus on lessons already learned. I trust that recognizing the truths in what was will lead to growth in what is. I constantly remind myself that:

1. Life comes in seasons
There's a time to plant, a time to nurture, and a time to harvest. No matter how quickly we want to move things along, we cannot rush life. It will happen when it happens, so don't bother fighting the flow. You'll only end up suffering.

2. There's always an end

No matter how miserable, unhappy, afraid, or impatient you get about a life situation, it too shall come to an end. Life is a state of flux and constantly in motion, even if we don't see it. Everything that has a beginning eventually has an end or transforms into something else.

3. Timing is everything

We live in a culture where instant gratification has become the norm, but I believe that if something is worth having, it's worth waiting for. The puzzle is more than the perfect, finished product at the end. Remember that at the beginning of every puzzle, all we can comprehend is that there is chaos; there are all these pieces scattered all over and we have no idea how they'll come together. The thing is, however, they *will* come together. At the right time, what didn't make sense eventually will. If all else fails, keep in mind that the waiting will also end. This is how life works after all.

THE BEAUTY AND MAGNIFICENCE OF THE SMALL STEPS

"Do not despise these small beginnings…"
—Zechariah 4:10

Before a child can walk, he or she has to crawl. The world's greatest philosophers, mathematicians, and spiritual leaders all took the baby steps of crawling on their hands and knees before standing on their two feet. We have been lectured on the importance of the future for so long that we have forgotten that the future is a culmination of steps taken in the Now. We forget that every thought, conversation, and connection is an important piece of the puzzle and that without these pieces, the puzzle cannot fully exist. Without these pieces, there is no big picture, no finished product.

"Pay attention to the steps you're taking towards
your goal. Those steps are even more important
than the goal itself because the steps towards
that goal determine the quality of the goal."
— Eckhart Tolle

Fulfillment lies in the future. This is a lie that has been perpetuated for as long as human beings have existed. It is such a common lie that many of us stopped recognizing it as an untruth and have embraced it as the norm. You have a goal, you work as hard as you possibly can, you achieve that goal, and then you'll be happy. Don't get me wrong; fulfillment and happiness can come in the future, but when you get "there," it won't be the future, it will once again be Now. Besides, most people who achieve their goals are usually met at the end with a sense of "what now?" The journey toward finding fulfillment begins again.

I received the best advice from my dad when I started my fashion blog a few years ago. I was so stressed about all the content I needed to produce and all the ideas that would or would not work and how they would work—the worry list was endless. After sensing all of the tension and anxiety brewing, he said I should quit. I was taken aback. This was coming from a man who had never quit anything in his life. What he said next is something that I go back to every day, "There are a million things you could be miserable doing, why be miserable doing what you love?"

All I could see was the destination—where I needed to be. I forgot to find joy in the process of discovery, in the exciting challenge of building something from scratch; I forgot to find beauty in every victory; I forgot to marvel at the magnificence of each step taken.

> "Gratitude unlocks the fullness of life. It turns what
> we have into enough, and more. It turns denial into
> acceptance, chaos to order, confusion to clarity.
> It can turn a meal into a feast, a house into a home,
> a stranger into a friend."
> —Melody Beattie

Who you are in the small steps is who you'll be at the end. If you're miserable on your journey to success, you don't all of a sudden become the Dalai Lama when you "make it." There's no automatic peace, Zen, and happiness that comes over you. Appreciating each moment along the way requires being present in those moments. It requires recognizing that no step is more or less important than the other.

I often remind myself that before a plant can bloom, a seed has to go underground. It is dark and scary underground, but it is a crucial step in what will be. Roots have to take their place, the seed has to be nurtured with water and light; all of these steps are key to the first bloom. The beauty that we see at the end cannot exist without those steps. There is no end without a beginning.

THE MAGNIFICENT POWER
OF GRATITUDE

The holiday season is my absolute favorite time of the year. It's not only a time to celebrate family, friends, and tradition, but it's also a time of reflection for most: a time to look back at all that the past year had to offer, both good and bad. For a lot of people, this time also draws focus to the things that are missing, the things that have been lost, and the things that we're still waiting for. It's very easy to lose sight of all that is while yearning for that which is to be.

What's also easy is telling everyone how much they have to be grateful for, without walking a mile in their shoes. During this time, I usually encounter a good number of people who are ready for the year to be over. They have been put through the wringer, they have become pessimistic, and they have lost hope. Many have decided to take a rest from the race, while others have simply quit altogether—they have no more fight in them.

I once read that "often, the happiest people in the world don't have the best of everything…they just make the best of everything." Depending on what your life situation is at this point in time, it may be harder for you than most to find a way to be grateful or to see the silver lining. What nature and, specifically, the change in seasons teaches us is that there is no such thing as permanence in life. This, too, will pass. Things change. Life changes. You change. It is inevitable.

Sometimes, life can be so challenging that you can't afford to take things one day at a time—you have to take things one minute at a time. When this is the case, it is an opportunity for you to rise above the reality you're in. By reaching for gratitude, instead of pain, you have shown that you are stronger than you think you are. I've actually found that as soon as I acknowledge that I'm grateful for anything, the load lightens up; I become a little less burdened and a bit freer. I realize that I'm better off than where I started.

> "There are only two ways to live your life. One is as though nothing is a miracle. The other is as though everything is a miracle."
> —Albert Einstein

As this holiday season begins, it's important to take the time to reflect on how far you've come in your journey. Take a moment or a few moments to be grateful for the path taken and for the unacknowledged victories. Remember that there are no good or bad experiences, just experiences. Most important, accept that each experience is an important piece of the puzzle. Know that each experience serves a purpose to grow and build you. Appreciate it. Embrace it. Be grateful for it.

CINDERELLA IS
A STATE OF MIND

At some point, we have all thought that someone or something could save us from the present moment. At some point, we have all believed that the future will make us happier, richer, and more fulfilled. Life situations and circumstances change, but who we are at our core does not.

> "We are not human beings having a spiritual experience. We are spiritual beings having a human experience."
> — Pierre Teilhard de Chardin

My friend currently works as a nanny. In the daytime, she's usually covered in dirt from the playground, food from mealtime, and a whole lot of depression, stress, and anxiety from the thoughts that haunt her about being stuck in a job that she would rather not be doing. In her dream life, she's an actor, writer, and producer. The truth is that it doesn't matter if she's a multihyphenate talent or a nanny. What she does is not who she is, and this is a fact that many of us forget. At parties, for example, instead of people asking about who a person is, the first thing they ask about is what a person does. That is how much our identities are tied to our professions and occupations. It does makes sense that we would mistake what we do for who we are—after all, most of us will spend an average of 90,360 hours working in our lifetime.

What I want to say to my friend is that who she is as a nanny is who she will be as an actor. I want to tell her that her insecurities won't suddenly disappear if she becomes famous —that money and opportunities won't fix a broken spirit. I want to tell her that the nanny job will end (because most jobs do), but so will acting/writing/producing eventually. What will remain is who she is.

Cinderella: Why, it's like a dream. A wonderful dream come true.

Fairy Godmother: Yes, my child, but like all dreams, well, I'm afraid this can't last forever. You have only until midnight, and —

Cinderella: Midnight? Oh, thank you —

Fairy Godmother: Oh, now, just a minute. You must understand, my dear: On the stroke of twelve, the spell will be broken, and everything will be as it was before.

Cinderella: Oh, I understand, but… it's more than I ever hoped for. (Cinderella, 1950).

At some point, we have all put power in the hands of a fairy godmother to transform our lives and, in turn, give us fulfillment. Our fairy godmother could come in the form of a new job, a new home, a new love, fame, or fortune. We believe that when we get what we want, we will be free, happy, and the best version of ourselves. But, what happens when the clock strikes midnight? What happens when the euphoria wears off and we're left to face what always remains—ourselves?

"Something in us knows, deep in the gut or the heart, perhaps at an unconscious level, that we are made of more than just the sum total of our thoughts, feelings and the life situation that we are living at the moment. We have a sense of being larger or more infinite than just our little 'me.' And for most of us, the idea that we humans are vaster than just finite and personal egos feels relieving, even if we can't quite access the knowing of it directly."
—Nancy Colier

Most human beings are imprisoned by the mind. The irony is

that we don't recognize that we're living our fancy lives out-side the walls. We search for peace and happiness everywhere and in everything while trapped between the past and the future, never acknowledging what's right in front of us—the present. It's like being born in an asylum. All you've ever known is crazy, so when you step outside and see what "nor-mal" looks like, your mind finds it difficult to comprehend.

"Know thyself…"

"When will I ever see the am that I am?" the poet Rumi once lamented. I can confidently say that who I am is a creator and a creative being. I am here to know myself through self-expression. There is no right or wrong way to do this, just signs, guiding and leading and helping to course correct. I am not what I do, although what I do can be an expression of who I am. What I do will change—often. Nothing lasts forever. I may choose to do something or choose to do nothing. I can be happy doing anything. Life has a rhythm; I choose to flow with it and never against it. My happy ending is not depen-dent on anything outside of me. It is here and it is now.

HAVE YOU FORGOTTEN?

What makes one person believe that they are worth everything and another feel like they are worth nothing? The environment we grow up in plays a huge part in forming our opinions on what we think we're worth, and so do the people we surround ourselves with. Ultimately, however, self-worth begins and ends with the self. No one can add or take away from who we truly are and certainly no words or actions can actually diminish the true self.

If this is the case, why do so many of us settle for less than we're worth? From unfulfilling jobs, marriages, and relationships to friendships that neither show respect nor value for who we are, what is it that makes it okay for us to rationalize the small way in which we view ourselves? My theory is that we've simply forgotten.

"Who do you think you are?"

I've heard the words "As a man thinketh, so is he" for most of my life. Ask someone about who they think they are and they'll rattle off words about their job, where they went to school, marital status, recent accolades, and so on. The interesting thing is that in spite of our fluctuating and rambling thoughts, who we truly are doesn't change. It never has and it never will. If an eagle is raised among chickens and begins to act like a chicken, if he never learns to fly, eats whatever he can find on the ground instead of soaring above its prey and snatching up the cream of the crop, if he settles for less than what he is worth, it's not because he stopped being an eagle, he simply forgot who he truly is.

Who you may think you are could change at any given time, based on your mood, financial status, age, societal expectations, and many other factors—which is why it's important to go beyond the mind and thoughts to remember. After all, "It wasn't through the mind, through thinking, that the miracle that is life on earth or your body were created and are being sustained" (Eckhart Tolle, *The Power of Now*).

"Who do you know you are?"

Knowing is the key. Some of us know in a big way, without doubt and with every ounce of certainty we can muster. For others, it's a small and still piece of us, a flickering light that refuses to go out in a sometimes dark and shapeless world. Whatever the size, knowing reminds us of what we've buried and what we've forgotten. Knowing reminds us of the greatness within—it reminds us of what we've felt inklings of but refuse to let ourselves believe. Knowing reminds us that the light within is so great that it can never be doused nor trampled upon by another.

It reminds us that we are beyond the nine-to-five, bills, shaky relationships, and our life situations. It reminds us that we are gifted and do have the power to shape our existence in collaboration with life. Most important, it reminds us that we are creative souls, part of the universal mind, choosing to have a human experience. The words "I AM" are probably the most powerful words you'll ever utter as a human being. Knowing floods those two words with light. Suddenly, we begin to truly live the life we deserve, the life we were always meant to live.

TIME TO SHOW UP FOR YOUR DREAMS

"The most regretful people on earth are those who felt the call to creative work, who felt their own creative power restive and uprising, and gave to it neither power nor time."

—Mary Oliver

I'm not afraid of dying. What I'm afraid of is dying with my dreams buried inside me. That is what I find terrifying. When I was little, I would stand in front of the mirror and ask myself, "Who am I?" I'd do this often. I'd stare for a few minutes and I could have sworn that I felt something deep, swirling, and powerful. I'd feel a little funny, light, and then stop. A few days later, I'd ask myself the same question again. At five years old, I could sense that I had a purpose. I wasn't sure exactly what the path would look like or what would be waiting at the end, but I knew something was brewing. That was enough then.

> "Most of us have two lives. The life we live,
> and the unlived life within us."
> — Steven Pressfield, *The War of Art*

They say the fastest way to get from Point A to Point B is a straight line, but the point of life is not to get through it as fast and as straight as we can. Life is messy. It is filled with many squiggly paths and these paths are the farthest thing from a straight line. Life is also very complicated, but a complicated life is no excuse to bury our dreams. I find it interesting that we show up for work every day to cash a paycheck no matter how complicated and messy our life situations are, but we refuse to show up for our dreams—we refuse to show up for our purpose. If your car broke down on your way to work, you would find another way to make it there, but one letter of rejection, one "no," and most of us will completely throw in the towel. What are we so afraid of?

> "Are you paralyzed with fear? That's a good sign.
> Fear is good. Like self-doubt, fear is an indicator.
> Fear tells us what we have to do."
> — Steven Pressfield, *The War of Art*

My mother often tells me that one of the things she loves about me is that I'm brave. She believes that I have spunk. I tell her that I'm always afraid but that I make my moves in spite of the fear, not because of it. We all experience fear. Sometimes, I experience fear of failure and success simultaneously. I actually use this as a compass. The more afraid I am of something, the more I know that I have to move in that direction. My experience tells me that fear is like a shadow. It's dark, looming, and intimidating, but it's just air, literally the space between where I am and the manifestation of my dreams.

Ten years ago, I moved to Los Angeles with no job or contacts and $1500 in my account. I was a recent graduate who left a full-time job on the East Coast with no prospect of another. Armed with a lot of faith and an equal amount of spunk, I embarked on a journey that I was so confident would change my life forever. I couldn't really explain what I felt in my gut to other people; I just knew.

We are all artists and creative souls in our own right and the world deserves to know us at our fullest potential. If you're thinking, "I don't even know where to start," be still. You already know the answer — where you start doesn't matter. Imagine you are a point on a circle: Whether you move forward or backward doesn't matter. You will invariably be led back to your origin — the source. Brainstorm, write down ideas, create and travel the path. Don't worry about creating a perfect path — the journey is the best part.

The simplest messages are often the most profound. Nike was on to this, which is why the slogan "Just do it" has lived on for so long. Just do it. Do something, anything that will lead you down the path you know deep inside you're supposed to experience. Listen to your soul's urge; it is the calm beneath the rocky current. Choose yourself and your dreams and show up for them. A writer is a writer the moment she writes a paragraph; a painter is a painter the moment he takes a brush to canvas. You are a creator the moment you create something. One step—that's all it takes.

> "For to everyone who has will more be given, and he will have an abundance. But from the one who has not, even what he has will be taken away…"
> —Matthew 25:29

We have all been endowed with gifts to enhance our human experience. We may think that individuals who are famous, recognized, or in the public eye have greater gifts than a teacher or a stay-at-home mom, but that's just an illusion. A farmer who refuses to plant his seed, no matter how small, for fear of failure is already a failure. He will never know what works and doesn't work; he will never master his soil or his seed and he will never know abundance.

WHEN WAS THE LAST TIME YOU LAUGHED?

"Always laugh when you can, it is cheap medicine."
—George Gordon Byron

It's been claimed that children laugh more than 300 times a day while adults laugh less than 20 times a day. Whether that number is accurate or not, what is evident is that there seems to be a shift as we grow into adulthood. We become so serious about life and forget why we're really here—to express ourselves with joy. We chase fortunes and advancement until we drive ourselves to the brink of exhaustion, depression, and failing health, then we spend our entire fortune trying to find ways to heal and turn back the damage we've caused. I'm a pretty happy person, but I often find myself so caught up in the stress of daily life that I forget to be present, to really feel the joy of being. Most of us are waiting for our lives to perfectly line up to finally be happy. We forget that happiness is relative.

"Once upon a time, an old farmer lived in a poor country village. His neighbors considered him well-to-do because he owned a horse, which he used for many years to work his crops. One day his beloved horse ran away. Upon hearing the news, his neighbors gathered to commiserate with him. 'Such bad luck,' they said sympathetically. 'Maybe,' the farmer replied. The next morning the horse returned but brought with it six wild horses. 'How wonderful,' the neighbors rejoiced. 'Maybe,' replied the old man. The following day, his son tried to saddle and ride one of the untamed horses, was thrown, and broke his leg. Again, the neighbors visited the farmer to offer their sympathy on his misfortune. 'Maybe,' said the farmer. The day after that, conscription officers came to the village to draft young men into the army. Seeing that the farmer's son had a broken leg, they passed him by. The neighbors congratulated the farmer on how well things had turned out. 'Maybe,' the farmer replied."
—Sonja Lyubomirsky, *The Myths of Happiness*

Unhappiness exists in everything that has the possibility of making us happy, it's part of the duality of life—a system of checks and balances. So, how do we find peace in unhappiness, grace in misery, and gratitude in uncertainty? I think laughter is the key. It softens the hard edges the mind has formed to protect itself, it breaks down barriers, and it instantly lightens the load of everyday life. I laugh a lot but even then, I often ask myself, "When was the last time you laughed?" Something happens when I do this: I immediately become conscious and aware of all that is happening around me and most especially within.

> "So many tangles in life are ultimately hopeless that
> we have no appropriate sword other than laughter."
> —Gordon W. Allport

Life is not easy and we often complicate things even more with unconscious actions. We surround ourselves with people, jobs, and situations that drain the life and the joy out of us. We spend most of our time worrying and being upset about things that may or may not happen, things that have happened, or things that we're afraid of. We spend our seconds and minutes fighting shadows. Laughter cuts though the darkness and the shadows. Physically, it also helps boost our mood; it helps relieve stress, stimulate many organs, and increase endorphins. Steve Wilson, the founder of The World Laughter Tour notes that "Muscular tension is released when you laugh. Your digestion is better. It helps heart rate. It helps blood flow."

"Nothing in life is as important as you think it is
while you are thinking about it."
—Daniel Kahneman

Our lives are a culmination of moments—not good and bad moments or important and insignificant moments—just pure moments. We often forget that each moment carries equal value and serves a purpose. When we fight or reject a moment, it's like a prisoner banging his head on the steel rods that surround him in an attempt to get out. The only thing getting dented is his head. Our goal should always be to honor each moment as it is, knowing that all is flux and always changing; our goal is to understand that freedom is a state of mind. Using laughter as a driver for inner peace, especially in times we view as tumultuous, is a very easy step to take, but then the world's most complicated questions often have very simple answers.

Hearing the laughter of a child is pure, unadulterated joy (literally and figuratively). I'm often in awe of the purity of those moments—untouched by what we've come to know as "life as it is," yet inspired by life itself in every way. I then realize that this is who we are at our core—not damaged or jaded or afraid or too busy with life to just be. We are pure, undiluted joy. It's important that we never forget that.

THE PATH IS MESSY

They say the fastest way from Point A to Point B is a straight line. This is always true in theory, but in real life and especially in our human experience, straight lines are rare. I've seen this trend in the lives of the great men and women whom I admire. Every good story is filled with twists and turns. It's what keeps the observer intrigued and wanting more. Getting to the end of the story is great, but the journey to the end is greater. The journey is what keeps us at the edge of our seats.

I often think about the twisted lines that connected Steve Jobs —the baby who was given up for adoption, menace in the third grade, college dropout, Zen seeking, fired founder—to Steve Jobs—the entrepreneur, businessman, and visionary. We look at his story and we are in awe of everything he achieved. No one can deny his brilliance or contributions, but what a messy story—a mentally, physically, emotionally, and spiritually messy story.

He was a visionary, but I'm almost positive that the vision wasn't clear when he was sleeping on the floor in friends' dorm rooms, returning Coke bottles at 5¢ each for food money, and getting weekly free meals at the local Hare Krishna temple. I'm sure the vision wasn't as clear as he traveled through India searching for spiritual enlightenment or when he was publicly ousted from the company he helped make a giant.

> "If you haven't found it yet, keep looking. Don't settle.
> As with all matters of the heart, you'll know when
> you find it. And, like any great relationship, it just
> gets better and better as the years roll on."
> —Steve Jobs

For most of us, it takes time to find the vision and even more time for it to take root and unfold. It's important to constantly remind ourselves that this is why we're here, to experience all of that time in its full glory—we are here to discover. There's a reason why we gravitate toward roller coasters and there's a reason why we enjoy the thrill of the highs and lows of those rides. It's all about creating a memorable experience. The same goes for our journey here; it's not about the final destination but all the moments that make up the whole experience.

"I don't believe in failure. It is not failure
if you enjoyed the process."
—Oprah Winfrey

Sometimes, it's okay not to know how or when or why. It took me a long time to be able to accept this. I finally realized that the journey lies between those words. When I was six, I discovered that I was a very persuasive speaker. I could argue my way out of anything. I decided that I would be a lawyer. From middle school all the way through college, there were debate teams, public speaking competitions, the law strand, and many mock trials. It's interestingly hazy, but somewhere between my senior year of college and my graduation, I refused to give the LSAT and law school any thought. I decided that there were so many other things that I was interested in pursuing, and I never looked back. It would take over a decade to filter through those interests, but I found my footing.

"Have the courage to follow your heart and
intuition, they somehow already know
what you want to become..."
—Steve Jobs

The path is messy. It is rarely straightforward. There will be ups and downs, trials, errors, and failures; there will be moments of fear and doubt, but there will also be many beautiful, unexpected surprises. Along the way, you will discover that you are not alone. You will discover that you've had an inner guide every step of the process. It started as a small, still voice, but the more you listened, the stronger it became, eventually having the ability to drown out all the outside noise.

In time, you will realize that there is no right or wrong way to walk this path, so it's pointless to model your experience after another's or to wish for another's life. You will learn that the best you can do is to be open and aware, to live consciously, with integrity and compassion for the journey, for others, but, most important, for yourself.

CUSTOM ORDERS

I believe there are two types of buyers: those who take things as is and those who prefer a customized version. When you go into a car dealership, you can take the car as you see it on the floor, or you can ask for leather seats, a change in color, a navigation system, stick shift or automatic transmission, or even heated seats. It all depends on what caters to your wants and needs. The same goes for the things we ask of life. We can either say "I'll take my order as is" or ask for a customization. Please note, however, that if you ask for a customization, the standard delivery time may not apply to your order because changes take time. The right job opportunity takes time, so does the right home, love, mentor, and business.

Because I'm in fashion, I'll use an example of ordering an Hermès bag. Did you know that customers may currently wait from six months to one year for the delivery of one of the house's signature bags? That's not all. With certain bags, the process of hand-stitching individual pieces with linen thread and using an awl can apparently take up to two years from creation to delivery (depending on your taste for luxurious leather and current demand for your coveted style).

So, what does this all mean? The next time you wonder where your soulmate is, why it didn't work out with your last boyfriend, even why you didn't get that job you interviewed so well for, please remember whether or not you put in a custom order. Remember whether you asked for just another job or one that would not only pay you well but also provide flexibility so that you can travel or spend more time with your family. Remember whether you asked for just another boyfriend or someone who would grow old with you and someone who would move heaven and earth to make you happy.

If you did put in a custom order, please know that nothing but the best is good enough for you. Know that it takes time to put your custom order together and don't forget to leave some room for finishing as well. Premium goods, unlike mass-produced things, require perfection. One last thing: Tell yourself over and over again that this exquisite order of yours will be right on time and will not go one second over life's intended delivery date. If we have the courage to ask for something special, we need to use that same courage to wait for it.

IT IS POSSIBLE BECAUSE
IT SEEMS IMPOSSIBLE

I've always been fascinated by the idea of "destiny versus free will." Is this all set or do we have a say? What if we mess things up? Can we even mess things up? I don't think any of us have the perfect answer for this, and perhaps it's because there is no perfect answer here and now. Perhaps destiny and free will work hand in hand to paint a glorious picture of the possibilities and capabilities of the human spirit. Perhaps it's not about one or the other but more about what the picture represents to us and for us — purpose.

I recently started binge-watching *The Crown* on Netflix. As I watched the first episode, which focuses on Princess Elizabeth and her wedding to the Duke of Edinburgh, Philip Mountbatten, I thought about another girl: a mixed-race girl, a divorcée, and a child of divorce herself, an American born in California but based in Toronto, an actress whose past credits include being a suitcase girl on *Deal or No Deal*. This girl would one day very soon walk onto the steps of Windsor Castle, with the entire world watching and become an integral part of the British monarchy.

Free Will…?

Ms. Meghan Markle is, of course, more than just a prince's fiancée. She's a Northwestern University graduate who pursued her dream and no matter how people categorize her career status, she did something that most dreamers don't get a chance to do in Hollywood—she became a working actress. In addition to a seven-year stint on the USA show *Suits*, she worked as an advocate for women and children, traveling to Rwanda for a clean water campaign and partnering with the United Nations Entity for Gender Equality and the Empowerment of Women. She also launched a lifestyle website called the Tig and became editor-in-chief.

As someone who has dreams of her own, I can imagine that in spite of the achievements listed above, Ms. Markle probably wanted more. She comes across as a driven young woman and I'm sure that even as she reported to the set of *Suits* every season, she was still working toward that breakthrough and that big break. I can imagine that even with her lifestyle website, she might have felt lost in a sea of bloggers and influencers as she tried to create something to make herself stand out. I can guarantee that she would never have dreamed that the platform she desired would show up in the form that it did nor the scale that it has. Well, that's the funny thing about destiny...

Destiny...?

Before Ms. Markle was King Edward VIII, who abdicated the throne to marry the twice-divorced American socialite, Wallis Simpson, thereby thrusting his brother, King George VI into the role. With King George's early death, Queen Elizabeth II took the throne at the tender age of 25, leading the way for her son, Prince Charles to someday take the throne. Part of his preparation for that role included marrying Princess Diana and producing heirs, Prince William and Prince Harry, which brings me back to Ms. Markle. She is more than a marriage and a spouse, but right now, that marriage has lunged and launched her into a space that nothing else—not acting or designing or blogging—could. Everything about where she ended up based on where she was coming from had impossible written all over it—yet her name will be written in the history books.

Ms. Markle tried to be an influencer among a sea of influencers —now the world watches her every move. Every product used, every piece of clothing worn is now followed, searched for, and copied. I'm sure her greatest desire at some point was for her acting career to create a prominent place for her in the world. She now has that prominent place and will have a chance to do more than just pose on the red carpet and answer questions about whom she's wearing. The world is now her stage and I can guarantee that her original dream is not even close to matching her current reality.

I've been told that there can only be hope where there's life, but I say that there can only be life where there's hope. Even if we don't want to admit it, even in the midst of our greatest challenges, we stand because there's a flicker of hope that exists in the midst of the darkness. We all have dreams, desires, and aspirations floating around in our psyche. Many times, they seem impossible, but it is because of that impossibility that I know they are possible. As long as there's hope, against all odds and because of the odds, with a little grace, the impossible suddenly becomes possible.

ABOUT THE AUTHOR

Wemi Opakunle is a motivational speaker and writer dedicated to the encouragement and empowerment of the human spirit. She has authored articles on the search for purpose, discovering the true self, and the end of suffering. Recognizing that none of the outer accomplishments we seek mean anything without consciousness and awareness, Wemi spends her time spreading the message of hope, finding spiritual balance, and encouraging others to live their lives to their fullest potential.

Based in Los Angeles, California, she was born in Nigeria and moved to the United States with her family at 13 years old. A graduate of the University of Maryland, College Park, with a bachelor's degree in Government & Politics and French, her childhood dream of becoming a lawyer was put on hold after graduation when she realized that she was being called to tread a path unbeaten.

She has since launched a fashion company, created a successful blog, appeared as a fashion expert in several media outlets, and interviewed quite a few of the industry's heavy hitters. She's also a tenured recruiter and currently discovers new talent for one of the world's most prominent entertainment brands.

Wemi is a dreamer and she believes in miracles.

WWW.THANKGODITSMONDAY.LIFE